Getting Organised

Ron Fry

KOGAN PAGE   SKB LIBRARY

Other books in this Kogan Page series:
How to Study
Improve Your Memory
Improve Your Reading
Improve Your Writing
Last Minute Study Tips

Forthcoming
Manage Your Time
Pass Any Test
Take Notes
Use Your Computer

First published in 1996 in the USA by The Career Press,
3 Tice Road, PO Box 687, Franklin Lakes, NJ 07417
This European edition published 1997 by Kogan Page Ltd

Kogan Page Limited
120 Pentonville Road
London N1 9JN

British Library Cataloguing in Publication Data

A CIP record for this book is available from the British Library.

ISBN 0 7494 2346 3

Typeset by Jo Brereton, Primary Focus, Haslington, Cheshire
Printed and bound in Great Britain by Clays Ltd St Ives plc

Contents

INTRODUCTION
Start at the beginning

Who are you?

A number of you are students, not just in secondary schools, but also college and university students.

Many of you reading this are adults. Some of you are returning to education; some of you left school a long time ago but have worked out that if you could learn now the study skills your teachers never taught you, you would do better in your careers – especially if you knew how to meet pressing deadlines or remember the key points of a presentation.

All too many of you are parents with the same lament: 'How do I get Johnny to do better in school? If his life is as organised as his room, I fear for all of us'.

I want to briefly take the time to address each one of the audiences for this book and discuss some of the factors particular to each of you.

If you are a secondary school student

You should be particularly comfortable with the format of the book – its relatively short sentences and paragraphs, occasionally humorous (hopefully) headings and subheadings and the language used. I wrote it with you in mind.

But you should also be uncomfortable with the fact that you are already in the middle of your school years – the period that will drastically affect, one way or the other, all the rest of your education – and you still do not know how to study! Don't lose another minute. Learning now how to organise your studying and your life is key to success now and in the future.

If you are a 'traditional' college or university student

Having left school and gone to college or university, learning how to organise your life and studies is not only a good idea, it is the only thing that will enable you to survive. Life will be busy... course schedules... volunteer schedule... athletics schedule... and work schedule.

If you are the parent of a student of any age

Your child's school is probably doing little if anything to teach him or her how to study, which means he or she is not learning how to learn. And that means he or she is not learning how to succeed.

What can parents do? There are probably even more dedicated parents out there than dedicated students. Here are the rules for parents of students of any age.

1 **Set up a homework area**. Free of distraction, well lit, all necessary supplies handy.

2 **Set up a homework routine**. When and where it gets done. Same start time every day.

3 **Set homework priorities**. Make the point that homework is the priority – before going out with friends, watching TV, whatever.

4 **Make reading a habit** – for them, certainly, but also for yourselves, if it is not already. Children will inevitably do what you do, not what you say.

5 **Turn off the TV**. Or, at the very least, severely limit the amount of TV watching you do.

6 **Talk to the teachers**. Find out what your children are supposed to be learning. If you do not, you cannot really supervise. You might be teaching them things at odds with what the teacher is trying to do.

7 **Encourage and motivate**, but do not nag them to do their homework. Nagging does not work.

8 **Supervise their work**, but do not fall into the trap of doing their homework for them.

9 **Praise them to succeed**, but do not overpraise them for mediocre work.

10 **Convince older students of reality**. Learning and believing that the real world does not care about their marks, but measures them solely by what they know and what they can do is a lesson that will save many tears, including yours.

11 **If you can afford it, get your children a computer** and all the software they can handle. Your children, whatever their age, must master computer technology in order to survive, let alone succeed, in and after school

The importance of your involvement

Do not for a minute underestimate the importance of your commitment to your child's success: your involvement in your child's education is absolutely essential to his or her eventual success.

So please, take the time to read this book. Learn what your children should be learning. You can help tremendously, even if you were not a brilliant student yourself, even if you never learned good study skills. You can learn now with your child – not only will it help him or her at school, it will also help you on the job, whatever your field.

If you are a non-traditional student

If you are going back to further education at the age of 25, 45, 65 or 85 – you probably need the help offered in _Getting Organised_, and the other books in this series, more than anyone. Why? Because the longer you have been out of education, the more likely it is that you do not remember what you have forgotten – and you have forgotten what you are supposed to remember. As much as I emphasise that it is rarely too early to learn good study habits, I must also emphasise that it is never too late.

If you are returning to education and attempting to carry even a partial course load while simultaneously holding down a job, raising a family, or both, there are some particular problems you face that you probably did not the first time you went to school.

Time and money pressures

Let's face it, when all you had to worry about was going to school, it simply had to be easier than going to college or university, bringing up a family and working for a living simultaneously. Mastering all of the techniques of time management is even more essential if you are to effectively juggle your many responsibilities to your career, family, clubs, friends, etc, with your commitment to education. Money management may well be another essential skill, how to pay for child care or how to manage all your responsibilities while cutting your hours at work to make time for college.

Self-imposed fears of inadequacy

You may well convince yourself that you are just 'out of practice' with all this college stuff. You do not even remember what to do with a highlighter. While some of this fear is valid, most is not; I suspect what many of you are really fearing is that you are not in that learning 'mentality' any more, that you do not 'think' the same way.

I think these last fears are groundless. You have been out there thinking and doing for quite a few years, perhaps very successfully, so it is ridiculous to think college or university will be so different. It will not be. Relax. You may have had a series of jobs, brought up a family, saved money, taken on more and more responsibility. Concentrate on how much more qualified you are for college now than you were then.

Feeling you are 'out of your element'

This is a slightly different fear, the fear that you just do not fit in any more. After all, you are not 18 again, but neither are many of the students at college today. Nowadays many college students are older than 25 and you will probably feel more in your element now than you did the first time around.

You will see teachers differently

It is doubtful you will have the same awe you did the first time around. At worst, you will consider teachers your equals. At best, you will consider them younger and not necessarily as successful or experienced as you are. In either event, you probably will not be quite as ready to treat your college or university lecturers as if they were akin to God.

There are differences in academic life

It is slower than the 'real' world, and you may well be moving significantly faster than its normal pace. When you were 18, an afternoon without lessons meant meeting your friends. Now it might mean catching up on a week's worth of errands, cooking (and freezing) a week's worth of dinners and/or writing four reports due last week. Despite your own hectic schedule, do not expect university life to accelerate in response. You will have to get used to people and systems with far less interest in speed.

Some random thoughts about learning

Learning should not be painful and certainly does not have to be boring, although it is far too often both. However, it is not necessarily going to be wonderful and painless, either, Sometimes you actually have to really apply yourself to work something out or get a project done. That is reality.

It is also reality that everything is not readily apparent or easily understandable and can cause confusion. Tell yourself that is okay and learn how to get past it. If you actually think you understand everything you have read the first time through, you are deluding yourself. Learning something slowly does not mean there is something wrong with you. It may be a subject that virtually everybody learns slowly.

A good student does not panic when something does not seem to be getting through the haze. He just takes his time, follows whatever steps apply and remains confident that the penny will eventually drop.

Parents often ask me, 'How can I motivate my teenager?' My initial response is usually to smile and say, 'If I knew the answer to that question, I would have retired very wealthy quite some time ago'. However, I think there is an answer, but it is not something parents can do, it is something you, the student, have to decide: are you going to spend the school day interested and alert or bored and resentful?

It is really that simple. Why not develop the attitude that you have to go to school anyway, so rather than being bored or miserable while you are there, you might as well be active and learn as much as possible? The difference between a C and an A or B for many students is, I firmly believe, merely a matter of wanting to do better. As I constantly stress in interviews, inevitably you will leave school, and very quickly, you will discover the premium is on what you know and what you can do. Marks will not count anymore, neither will exams results. So you can learn it all now or regret it later.

How many times have you said to yourself, 'I do not know why I am even trying to learn this (calculus, algebra, geometry, physics, chemistry, history, whatever). I will never use this again'? Remember, you have no idea what you are going to need to know tomorrow or next week, let alone next year or in the next decade.

I have been amazed in my own life how things I did with no specific purpose in mind (except probably earning money) turned out years later to be not just invaluable to my life or career but essential. How was I to know when I took German as my language choice in secondary school that the most important international trade show in book publishing, my field, was in Frankfurt... Germany? Or that the basic skills I learned one year working for an accountant (while I was writing my first book) would become essential when I later started four companies? Or how important basic maths skills would be in selling and negotiating over the years?

So learn it all. Do not be surprised if the subject you think is least likely to ever be useful ends up being the key to your fame and fortune.

Do it your way

You will find a plethora of techniques, tips, tricks, gimmicks and what-have-yous, some or all of which may work for you, some of which may not. Pick and choose, change and adapt, work out what works for you, because you are the one responsible for creating your study system, not me.

Occasionally I will point out 'my way' of doing something. I may even suggest that I think it offers some clear advantages to all the alternative ways of accomplishing the same thing, but that does not mean it is carved in stone.

I have used the phrase 'Study smarter, not harder' as a sort of catch-phrase for this series of books. What does it mean to you? Does it mean I guarantee you will spend less time studying? Or that the least amount of time is best? Or that studying is not ever supposed to be hard?

Hardly. It does mean that studying inefficiently is wasting time that could be spent doing other (probably more enjoyable) things and that getting your studying done as quickly and efficiently as possible is a realistic, worthy and attainable goal. I am no stranger to hard work, but I try not to work harder than I have to.

In case you were wondering

Before we get on with all the tips and techniques necessary, let me make an important point about this series of study books.

I believe in gender equality, in writing as well as in life. Unfortunately, I find constructions such as 'he or she', 's/he', 'womyn' and other such stretches to be sometimes painfully awkward. I have therefore attempted to sprinkle pronouns of both genders throughout the text.

I have attempted to create a system that is usable, that is useful, that is practical, that is learnable. One that you can use – whatever your age, whatever your level of achievement, whatever your IQ – to start doing better in school, in work and in life immediately.

1 The need for organisation

Whether you are a secondary school student just starting to feel frazzled, a college or university student juggling five modules and a part-time job, or a parent working, attending classes and bringing up a family, a simple, easy-to-follow system of organisation is crucial to your success. Despite your natural tendency to proclaim that you just do not have the time to spend scheduling, listing and recording, it is also the best way to give yourself more time.

Taking time to make time

I am sure many of you reading this are struggling with your increasing responsibilities and commitments. Some of you may be so overwhelmed you have just given up. Those of you who have not probably think it is your fault – if you just worked harder, spent more time on your essays and assignments, set up camp in the library – then everything would work out.

So you resign yourselves to all-night sessions, cramming for exams and forgetting about time-consuming activities like eating and sleeping. Trying to do everything – even when there is too much to do – without acquiring the skills to control your time, is an approach that will surely lead to burnout.

When does it all end?

With lessons, homework, a part-time or full-time job, and all the opportunities for fun and recreation, life as a student can be very busy. But, believe me, it does not suddenly get easier when you graduate.

Most adults will tell you that it only gets busier. There will always be a boss who expects you to work later, children who need to be fed, clothed and taken to the doctor, hobbies and interests to pursue, community service to become involved in, courses to take, etc.

If you are an adult doing all of the latter, I am sure I do not have to tell you how important organisation is, do I?

There may not be enough time for everything

When I asked one busy student if she wished she had more time, she joked, 'I'm glad there are only 24 hours in a day. Any more and I wouldn't have an excuse for not getting everything done.'

Let me give you the good news: there is a way that you can accomplish more in less time – and it does not take more effort. You can plan ahead and make conscious choices about how your time will be spent, and how much time you will spend on each task. You can have more control over your time, rather than always running out of time as you keep trying to do everything.

Now the bad news. The first step to managing your time should be deciding just what is important... and what is not. Although difficult, sometimes it is necessary for us to recognise that we really cannot do it all and we need to slice from our busy schedules those activities that are not as meaningful to us so that we can devote more energy to those that are. You may be a long-term Star Trek fan, but is it really the best use of your time to run back to your room to watch all the repeats?

You may love music so much, you want to be in the school orchestra, jazz band, choir and play with your own band on weekends. But is it realistic to commit to all four?

Your job at the new boutique may mean you get 20 per cent off all the clothes you buy. But if you are working there four days a week, have 15 hours of lessons and working at the supermarket on weekends, when do you expect to study?

If you are bringing up a family, working part time and trying to attend a part-time degree course yourself, it is probably time to cure yourself of the Superwoman syndrome.

But there is enough time to plan

Yet, even after paring down our commitments, most of us are still struggling to get it all done. What with lessons, study time, work obligations, extracurricular activities and social life, it is not easy fitting it all in – even without Star Trek.

The organisational plan that I outline in this book is designed particularly for students. Whether you are at secondary school, college or university, a 'traditional' student or one who has chosen to return to education after being out in the 'real world' for a while, you will find that this is a manageable programme that will work for you.

This programme allows for flexibility and I encourage you to adapt any of my recommendations to your own unique needs. That means it will work for you whether you are sharing accommodation with a roommate, living at home, or living with a partner and children. You can learn how to balance school, work, fun and even family obligations.

The purpose of this book is to help you make choices about what is important to you, set goals for yourself, organise and schedule your time and develop the motivation and self-discipline to follow your schedule and reach those goals, which will give you the time to learn all the other study skills I write about.

Wouldn't it be nice to have some extra time… instead of always running out of it?

To feel that you are exerting some control over your schedule, your school or college work, your life… instead of dashing from appointment to appointment, lesson to lesson, assignment to assignment, like some crazy snooker ball?

It can happen.

I will not spend a lot of time trying to convince you that this is a 'fun' idea – getting excited about calendars and to-do lists is a bit too much to hope for. You will not wake up one morning and suddenly decide that organising your life is the most fun thing you can think of.

But I suspect you will do it if I can convince you that effective organisation will reward you in some very tangible ways.

Presuming all this is true (and I bet it is), unless you have some very good reasons – a solid idea of some of the benefits effective organisation can bring you – you will probably find it hard to consistently motivate yourself to do it. It has to become a habit, something you do without thinking, but also something you do no matter what.

More work, less time, more fun!

An organisational or time management system that fits your needs can help you get more work done in less time. Whether your priority is more free time than you have now or improved marks, learning how to organise your life and your studies can help you reach your objective.

1 **It helps you put first things first**. Have you ever spent an evening busily doing an assignment for an easy course, only to find that you had not spend enough time studying for a crucial exam in a more difficult one?

Listing all the tasks you are required to complete and prioritising them ensures that the most important things will always get done – even on days when you do not get everything done.

2 **It helps you avoid time traps**. Time traps are the unplanned events that pop up, sometimes (it seems) every day. They are the fires you have to put out before you can turn to tasks like studying.

You may fall into such time traps because they seem urgent... or because they seem fun. Or you may end up spending hours in them... without even realising you are stuck.

There is no way to avoid every time trap. But effective time management can help you avoid most of them. Time management is like a fire-prevention approach rather than a fire-fighting one. It allows you to go about your work systematically instead of moving from crisis to crisis or from whim to whim.

3 **It helps you anticipate opportunities**. In addition to helping you balance study time with other time demands, effective time management can help make the time you do

spend studying more productive. You will be able to get more done in the same amount of time or (even better) do more work in less time. I am sure you could find some way to spend those extra hours each week.

Imagine that you and another student are working on the same big assignment. You plan out the steps to be completed well in advance and start on them early. The other student delays even thinking about the assignment until a week before it is due to be handed in.

If both of you were unable to find all the materials you needed in the local library, you, who started early, would have the opportunity to send away for them. The student who had only a week left would not have the same luxury, or the same good mark.

4 **It gives you freedom and control**. Contrary to many students' fears, time management is liberating, not restrictive. A certain control over part of your day allows you to be flexible with the rest of your day.

In addition, you will be able to plan more freedom into your schedule. For example, you would know well in advance that you have an important exam the day after a friend's party. Instead of having to ring your friend the night of the party with a sob story, you could make sure you allocate enough study time beforehand and go to the party without feeling guilty, without even thinking about the exam.

5 **It helps you avoid time conflicts**. Have you ever lived the following horror story? You finish a seminar at 5.30pm, remember you have an essay due in the next day, then realise you have no time to do it as you have a music rehearsal at 6pm. Then you remember that your football game is planned for 7pm... just before that evening engagement you organised months ago (which you completely forgot about until you came home and found a not-so-subtle message on your answering machine).

Simply having all of your activities, responsibilities and tasks written down in one place helps ensure that two or three things do not get scheduled at once. If time conflicts do arise, you will notice them well in advance and be able to rearrange things accordingly.

6 **It helps you avoid feeling guilty**. When you know how much studying has to be done and have the time scheduled to do it, you can relax – you know that the work will get done. It is much easier to forget about studying if you have already allotted the time to it. Without a plan to finish the work you are doing, you may feel like it is 'hanging over your head' even when you are not working on it. If you are going to spend time thinking about studying, you might as well just spend the time studying.

Effective time management also helps keep your conscience off your back. When your studying is done, you can really enjoy your free time without feeling guilty because you are not studying.

7 **It helps you evaluate your progress**. If you know where you should be in course readings and assignments, you will never be surprised when deadlines loom. For example, if you have planned out the whole term and know you have to read an average of 75 pages a week to keep up in your business management course, and you only read 60 pages this week, you do not need a calculator to work out that you are slightly behind. So it is easy enough to schedule a little more time to read next week so you can catch up on your schedule.

On the other hand, if you only read when it does not cut into your leisure time (ie, when your assignment does not conflict with your favourite TV programmes) or until you are tired, you will never know whether you are behind or ahead (but I will bet you are behind). Then one day you suddenly realise you have to be up to Chapter 7... by lunchtime.

8 **It helps you see the big picture**. Effective time management provides you with a bird's-eye view of the term. Instead of being caught off guard when the busy times come, you will be able to plan ahead – weeks ahead – when you have main exams or project assignments due for more than one course.

Why not complete that German literature essay a few days early so it is not in the way when two other essays are due… or when you are trying to get ready for a weekend camping trip? Conflicts can be worked out with fewer problems if you know about them in advance and do something to eliminate them.

9 **It helps you see the bigger picture**. Planning ahead and plotting your course early allows you to see how lessons fit in with your overall school and further education career. For example, if you know you have to take chemistry, biology and physics to be eligible for entrance into medical school, and the courses you will take later will build on those, you will at least be able to see why the lessons are required for your A levels, even if you are not particularly fond of one or two of them.

10 **It helps you learn how to study smarter, not harder**. Students sometimes think time management only means reallocating their time – spending the same time studying, the same time in class, the same time partying, just shifting around these time segments so everything is more 'organised'.

This is only partially true – a key part of effective time management is learning how to prioritise tasks. But this simple view ignores one great benefit of taking control of your time: it may be possible you will become so organised, so prioritised, so in control of your time that you can spend less time studying, get better marks and have more time for other things – extracurricular activities, hobbies, a film, whatever.

It is not magic, though it can appear magical.

It keeps getting better

Besides helping you to manage your time right now and reach your immediate study goals, learning how to organise your studying will continue to pay off.

Have you ever sat in a class and thought to yourself, 'I can't wait to leave school and forget all this stuff'?

You would not say that about organisational skills. They will be useful throughout your life. Preparation is what full-time education is all about – if you spend your time effectively now, you will be better prepared for the future.

Also, the better prepared you are, the more options you will have – effective learning and good marks now will increase your range of choices when you leave school. The company you work for or the university you attend will be one you choose, not one whose choice was dictated by your poor past performance.

Learning how to manage your time now will develop habits and skills you can use outside full-time education. It may be difficult for you to develop the habits of effective time management, but do not think you are alone – time manage-ment presents just as much of a problem to many parents, teachers and non-students. How many people do you know who never worry about time?

If you learn effective time management skills at school, the pay-offs will come throughout your life. Whether you end up running a household or a business, you will have learned skills you will use every day.

These techniques are tools that can be used to help you reach your short-term and long-range goals successfully. The important thing to remember is that you can be a successful time manager and a successful student if you are willing to make the effort to learn and apply the principles in this book.

If you hate the idea of being tied to a schedule, if you fear that it would drain all spontaneity and fun from your life, I know you will be pleasantly surprised when you discover that just the opposite is true.

Most students are relieved and excited when they learn what a liberating tool time management can be.

Let us explode some myths that may be holding you back.

Do I have to live at the library?

Learning effective organisational skills will not turn you into a study-bound bookworm. How much time do you need to set aside for studying? Ask your personal tutor, and he or she will probably echo the timeworn 2 : 1 ratio – spend two hours studying for each lesson for every hour you spend in the lesson.

Rubbish. That ratio may be way out of line – either not enough time or too much. The amount of study time will vary from individual to individual, depending on your lessons, abilities, needs and goals.

Scheduling time to study does not mean that you have to go from three hours of studying a day to eight. In fact, planning out your study time in advance often means you can relax more when you are not studying because you will not be worrying about when you are going to get your homework done – the time has been set aside.

How long you study is less important than how effective you are when you do sit down to study. The goal is not to spend more time studying, but to spend the same or less time, getting more done in whatever time you spend.

It is too complicated

Many fear that time management implies complexity. Actually, I recommend simplicity. The more complex your system, the harder it will be to use and, consequently, the less likely that you will use it consistently. The more complex the system, the more likely that it will collapse.

It's too inflexible

You can design your time management system to fit your own needs. Some of the skills you will learn in this book will be more helpful to you in reaching your goals than others. You may already be using some of them. Others you will want to start using immediately, while others may not fit your needs at all.

Use the skills that are most likely to lead you to your study goals, meet your needs and fit with your personality.

Inflexibility is most people's biggest fear – 'If I set it all out on a schedule, then I will not be able to be spontaneous and choose what to do with my time later'.

Your time management system can be as flexible as you want. In fact, the best systems act as guides, not some rigid set of 'must do's' and 'can't do's'.

That is enough about the myths. Let's take a look at what is actually required to use your time management skills effectively.

A good notebook and a sharp pencil

You have to be able to look at your plan when it's time to use it. It is nearly impossible to make detailed plans very far in advance without having a permanent record. Make it your rule – 'If I plan it out, I will write it down'.

Make sure that you have one place to write and keep all your schedule information, including lesson times, meetings, study times, project handing-in dates, holidays, doctor's appointments, social events, etc, so you always know exactly where to find them.

Your readiness to adapt and personalise

The time management system that best suits you will be tailor-made to fit your needs and personality.

Consider the following example. While most parents turn the lights out and keep things quiet when their baby is trying to go to sleep, one baby I know, who spent two months in the hustle and bustle of a new-born intensive care unit, could not sleep unless the lights were on and it was noisy.

Similarly, while many students will study best in a quiet environment, others may feel uncomfortable in a 'stuffy' library and prefer studying in their living room.

Make your study schedule work for you, not your night-owl roommate who must plan every activity down to the minute. Alter it, modify it, make it stricter, make it more flexible. Whatever works for you

You will never be disorganised again!

We have all had the experience of missing an important appointment or commitment and saying, 'I know I had that written down somewhere – I wonder where?'

It is easy to think, 'I'll write it down so I will not forget', but a schedule that is not used regularly is not a safety net at all. You must consistently write down your commitments. You must spend time filling out your schedule every week, every day.

Any efforts you make to manage your time will be futile if you do not have your schedule with you when you need it. For example, you are in an art lesson without your schedule when your teacher tells you when your next project has to be handed in. You jot it down in your art notebook and promise yourself you will add it to your schedule as soon as you get home.

You hurry to your next lesson, and your geology lecturer schedules a study session for the following week. You scribble a reminder in your lab book.

Between lessons, a friend stops to invite you to a party on Thursday night. You promise you will be there.

You arrive at work to find out your supervisor has scheduled your hours for the following week. She checks them with you, they seem fine, so you agree to do them.

Had you been carrying your schedule with you, you would have been able to write down your art project and schedule the necessary amount of preparation time.

You would have realised that your geology study session was the same night as your friend's party and discovered that accepting the work schedule your supervisor presented left you with little time to work on your art project.

Take your schedule with you anywhere and everywhere you think you might need it.

When in doubt, take it along!

Keeping your schedule with you will reduce the number of times you have to say, 'I'll just try to remember it for now' or 'I will write it down on this little piece of paper and transfer it to my planner later'.

Always make a point of writing down tasks, assignments, phone numbers and other bits of important information in your schedule immediately.

Use your new system consistently

In order to test its effectiveness, you must give any time management system a chance to work – give it a trial run. No programme can work unless it is utilised consistently. And consistency will not happen without effort.

It is just like learning to ride a bicycle. It is a pain at first; you may even fall off a few times. But once you are a two-wheel pro, you can travel much faster and farther than you could by foot.

The same goes for the techniques you will learn here – they may take practice and a little getting used to, but once you have lived a 'reorganised' life for a couple of weeks, you will probably find yourself in the habit of doing it. From then on, it will take relatively little effort to maintain.

That is when you will really notice the pay-off – when the task becomes second nature.

Organise your life

In one of my all-time favourite Abbott and Costello routines, the hapless Costello stands in front of a huge rolltop desk. There are hundreds, no thousands, of papers spilling out of it. Suddenly, Abbott, the supreme delegator, comes in and asks for 'the Smerling contract, 1942'. Costello pulls out a pair of enormous tongs, roots around in the cavernous desk, papers spilling everywhere, and pulls out a single sheet of paper. 'Smerling contract, 1942', he announces.

Many of us are probably just as disorganised as Costello's 'filing system', although I suspect more than a few of us would contend that we *can* find things in the clutter we like to call a desk. Whether we are kidding ourselves or not, becoming more organised in our lives – whether we are students, homebodies or career-ladder climbers – is the key to succeeding at home, at school and on the job.

Why things don't get done

Are you frustrated at the end of the day? Is your 'to do' list nearly as long at the end of the day as it was at the beginning? Do you sometimes feel you have spent all day going round in circles? Nearly all productivity problems can be traced to one or more of the items on the following list.

▮ **No clear goals**. Without a specific sense of purpose, it is impossible to effectively manage and organise your priorities. If you do not know where you are going, any road will take you there.

▮ **Lack of priorities**. The best to do list ever written is useless if it has not been prioritised. Most people naturally work on the easy or 'fun' things first. They may cross off a majority of their list, but miss the most important items.

Test your planning power

To learn something about your present orientation to planning do this questionnaire adapted from Jonathan and Susan Clark's *Make the Most of Your Workday* (Career Press, 1994), circling the answer that describes your orientation: 3 – agree, 2 – not sure, 1 – disagree.

I take regular time for planning every day	3	2	1
I have a personally chosen calendar or organisational system	3	2	1
I prioritise all my assignments... daily	3	2	1
I usually complete a daily schedule (see p47)	3	2	1
I do not have difficulty making decisions	3	2	1
I work daily on parts of projects due more than a week from now	3	2	1
The petrol tank in my car is presently at least half full	3	2	1
I know exactly when my most productive time of day is	3	2	1
I know my most important assignment for tomorrow	3	2	1
I have a current project board (see p43)	3	2	1

How did you do?

25 or more	You have a plan, and are working on it.
15–24	Sometimes your day gets the better of you.
Less than 15	How are you managing in this crisis?

■ **No daily plan**. Beginning your day without a plan of action is a formula for spending all day doing the wrong things. It invites anyone and everyone to interrupt your activities. You will passively allow unwelcome intrusions, because you will have no way to defend yourself.

■ **Perfectionism**. Are you unable to complete and hand in an assignment (essay, lab report, presentation, whatever) until it is done perfectly? Can you still see ways for something to be done better? Even if you cannot see anything, does it nag you that there must be something you overlooked?

- **Personal disorganisation**. No matter how organised your priorities or how effective your daily plan, you may be losing irretrievable time searching for things that are lost in the mess on your desk, in your files, cupboards and even your car.

- **Interruptions**. Your day can be going according to schedule… until a friend drops in or a game of five-a-side football begins. Many of these events can be eliminated; those that cannot must be controlled.

- **Procrastination**. It always seems like a good idea to 'put off today what you can do tomorrow'. After all, tomorrow is another day. But it catches up with you.

If some or all of these apply to you, it is time to change some habits. If you are determined to do so, I have some good news. Not only can bad habits be broken, but they can be replaced by good habits relatively easily. In fact, it is much easier to replace a habit than to break it. Just replace the 'sloth habit' with the good organisational habits in this book. Here is your battle plan.

- **Begin today**. The best time to start working on your resolve to be better organised is today. Do not procrastinate. Your motivation and resolve will not be stronger in a month than they are now. Start now and set a goal to acquire this new habit within the next 30 days.

- **Spread the word**. Do not keep your resolve a secret. Commit yourself to positive change by telling your friends and family what you have decided to do and by challenging them to keep you to your commitment.

- **Practise, practise, practise**. Practice is the motor oil that lubricates any habit's engine. The more you do something, the more ingrained it becomes.

The goal pyramid

One way to visualise all your goals – and their relationship to each other – is to construct a goal pyramid. Here is how to do it.

1 Centred at the top of a piece of paper, write down what you hope to ultimately gain from your education. This is your long-range goal and the pinnacle of your pyramid.

2 Below your long-range goal(s), list mid-range goals – milestones or steps that will lead you to your eventual target.

3 Below the mid-range goals, list as many short-range goals as you can – smaller steps that can be completed in relatively short periods of time.

Change your goal pyramid as you progress through education. You may eventually decide on a different career. Or your mid-range goals may change as you decide on a different path leading to the long-range goal. The short-range goals will undoubtedly change, perhaps daily.

The process of creating your own goal pyramid allows you to see how all those little daily and weekly steps you take can lead to your mid-range and long-term goals, and will motivate you to work on your daily and weekly tasks with more energy and enthusiasm.

Make goal-setting a part of your life

The development of good study skills is the route to your goals, whatever they are. No matter how hard you have to work or how much adversity you have to overcome along the way, the journey will indeed be worth it.

How do you make setting goals a part of your life? Here are some hints that may help.

1 **Be realistic when you set goals**. Do not aim too high or too low and do not be particularly concerned when (not if) you have to make adjustments along the way.

2 **Be realistic about your expectations**. An improved understanding of a subject you have little aptitude for is preferable to getting hopelessly bogged down if its total mastery is impossible.

3 **Do not give up too easily**. You can be overly realistic – too ready to give up just because something is a trifle harder than you would like. Do not aim too high and feel miserable when you do not come close, or aim too low and never achieve your potential – find the path that is right for you.

4 **Concentrate on areas that offer the best chance for improvement**. Unexpected successes can do wonders for your confidence and might mean you achieve more than you thought you could, even in other areas.

5 **Monitor your achievements and keep resetting your goals**. Daily, weekly, monthly, yearly – ask yourself how you have done and where you would like to go now.

How perfect are you?

Perfectionists care perhaps too much, finding it impossible to be satisfied with anything less than 'perfect' work (as they define it), presuming that such an ideal can actually be attained.

It is possible, of course, to score a perfect 100 in an exam or to get an A+ for an essay the teacher calls 'perfect' in the margin. But in reality, doing anything perfectly is an impossible task.

What does all this have to do with you? Nothing, unless you find yourself spending two hours polishing an already A+ essay or half an hour searching for that one perfect word or an hour rewriting good notes to make them absolutely perfect. In other words, while striving for perfection may well be a noble characteristic, it can very easily (perhaps inevitably) turn into a major problem if it becomes an uncontrollable and unstoppable urge that seriously inhibits your enjoyment of your work and your life.

If you really would prefer spending another couple of hours polishing that A+ essay to seeing a film, reading a book or getting some other assignment done, be my guest. Is the last 10 per cent or so really worth it? In some cases it is, but not usually.

Three more rules to help you get organised

As you begin to make goal-setting and organisation a part of your daily life, here are three concepts that will make a huge difference in your success.

Small changes, over time, make a big difference

A simple, tiny change in your behaviour may have virtually negligible results, but make hundreds of small changes, and the effects can be earth shattering.

Make this rule an automatic part of your thought process and your actions. It will help you understand the often small difference between success and failure, productivity and frustration, happiness and agony. It is so simple it is deceptive. Maybe just a little more training. Maybe a slightly better method of planning. Maybe just one tiny habit overcome. Maybe all of these and more. Each one alone is almost inconsequential, but when added up, the advantage is incredible.

The 80–20 Rule (Pareto Principle)

Another rule that you can apply to make a difference in how well you organise and manage your priorities is the 80–20 Rule, also known as the Pareto Principle.

Victor Pareto was an Italian economist and sociologist at the turn of the 20th century who studied the ownership of land in Italy. Pareto discovered that more than 80 per cent of all the land was owned by less than 20 per cent of the people. As he studied other things that people owned (including money), he found the same principle held true: 20 per cent or less of the people always ended up with 80 per cent or more of whatever he measured.

The most astonishing revelation about the 80–20 Rule is its opposite side. If 20 per cent of activities are producing 80 per cent of the results, then the other 80 per cent of activities are, in total, only giving 20 per cent of the results.

Remember. To apply the 80–20 Rule to manage your priorities, remind yourself that 20 per cent of the activities on your list are going to produce 80 per cent of the results and pay-off. Your question must constantly be, 'Which activities are the 20 percenters?'

Take advantage of 'in-between' time

You can become more productive by identifying the little windows of opportunity that pass through your life each day. They arrive unannounced and if you are not alert to them they will slip past you. What must you do with this 'in-between' time? Recognise it as soon as it occurs and use it immediately by taking premeditated action. If you do not have a plan, you will waste this time.

Here are some suggestions.

- Make phone calls.

- Read something.

- Post letters.

- Go the supermarket (or make your shopping list).

- Clear your desk and return things to their proper places.

- Review your daily schedule and reprioritise, if necessary.

- Go through your post.

- Write a quick note or letter home.

- Proofread some or all of one of your essays or assignments.

- Think (about a future assignment, an essay you are writing, etc).

- Relax.

3 *Organise your studying*

You can study more effectively. You can put in less time and get better results. However, learning how to do so is hard, because learning of any kind needs discipline, and learning self-discipline is, to many of us, the most difficult task of all.

If you are currently doing little or nothing in the way of formal learning, then you are going to have to put in more time and effort. How much more? Or even more generally, how long should you study for? Until you get the results you want to achieve.

The more effective you are and the more easily you learn and adapt the techniques in this book, the more likely you are to spend less time on your homework than before. But the further you need to go – from Ds to As rather than from Bs to As – the more you need to learn and the longer you need to give yourself to learn it.

Do not get discouraged. You will see results surprisingly quickly.

Get ready for a lifelong journey

Learning how to study is really a long-term process. Once you undertake the journey, you will be surprised at the number of landmarks, paths, side streets and road signs you will find. Even after you have transformed yourself into a better student than you had ever hoped to be, you will inevitably find one more signpost that offers new information, one more path that leads you in an interesting new direction. Consider learning how to study as a lifelong process and be ready to modify anything you are doing as you learn other methods.

This is especially important right from the start when you consider your overall study strategies. How long you study each night, how long you work on a particular subject and how often you schedule breaks are going to vary considerably depending on how well you were doing before you read this book, how far you have to go, how interested you are in getting there, how involved you are in other activities, the time of day, your general health, etc.

It gets more complicated: what is your study sequence? Hardest assignments first? Easiest? Longest? Shortest? Are you comfortable switching back and forth from one to another or do you prefer to focus on a single assignment from start to finish?

This gets even more difficult when you consider that the tasks themselves may have a great effect on your schedule. Fifteen-minute study units might work well for you most of the time (although I suspect half an hour is an ideal unit for most people, an hour only for those of you who can work that long without a break and who have assignments that traditionally take that long to complete).

On the other hand, you may have no problem at all working on a long project in fits and starts, 15 or 20 minutes at a time, without needing to retrace your steps each time you pick it up again.

What is the lesson in all of this? There is no ideal answer, certainly no 'right' answer, to many of the questions I have posed. It is a message you will read in these pages over and over again: find out what works for you and keep on doing it. If it later stops working or does not seem to be working as well, change it.

None of the organisational techniques discussed at length in this book is carved in stone. You should feel free to adapt and shape and bend them to your own needs.

Creating your study environment

On page 29, there is a checklist for you to rate your study environment. It includes not only where you study – at home, in the library, at a friend's – but also when and how you study. Once you have identified what works for you, avoid those situations in which you know you do not perform well. If you do not know the answer to one or more of the questions, take some time to experiment.

My Ideal Study Environment

How I receive information best:

1 ☐ Orally   ☐ Visually

In the classroom, I should:

2 ☐ Concentrate on taking notes
   ☐ Concentrate on listening

3 ☐ Sit in front ☐ Sit at the back ☐ Sit near window or door

Where I study best:

4 ☐ At home   ☐ In the library   ☐ Somewhere else

_____

When I study best:

5 ☐ Every night; little on weekends ☐ Mainly on weekends
   ☐ Spread out over seven days

6 ☐ In the morning   ☐ Evening   ☐ Afternoon

7 ☐ Before dinner   ☐ After dinner

How I study best:

8 ☐ Alone   ☐ With a friend   ☐ In a group

9 ☐ Under time pressure   ☐ Before I know I have to

10 ☐ With music   ☐ In front of TV   ☐ In a quiet room

11 ☐ Organising an entire night's studying before I start
    ☐ Tackling and completing one subject at a time

I need to take a break:

12 ☐ Every 30 minutes or so   ☐ Every hour
    ☐ Every 2 hours   ☐ Every _____ hours

Study groups: what are friends for?

The idea is simple: find a small group of like-minded students and share notes, question each other, prepare for exams together. To be effective, obviously, the students you pick to be in your group should share all, or at least most, of your lessons or courses.

Even if you find only one or two other students willing to work with you, such cooperation will be invaluable, especially in preparing for major exams.

Tips for forming your own study group

∎ I suggest four students minimum, probably six maximum. You want to ensure everyone gets a chance to participate while maximising the collective knowledge and wisdom of the group.

∎ While group members need not be best friends, nor should they be overtly hostile to one another. Seek diversity of experience, demand common dedication.

∎ Try to select students who are at least as clever, committed and serious as you. That will encourage you to keep up and challenge you a bit. Avoid a group in which you are the 'star' – at least until you flicker out during the first exam.

∎ Avoid inviting members who are inherently unequal – boyfriend/girlfriend combinations, in which one may be inhibited by the other's presence; situations where one student works for another; situations where 'underdogs' (underachievers) and 'brainies' may stifle one another; etc.

∎ Decide early on if you are forming a study group or a social group. If the latter, do not pretend it is the former. If the former, do not just invite your friends and sit around discussing your teachers.

∎ There are a number of ways to organise. My suggestion is to assign each course to one student. That student must master that assigned course, doing, in addition to the regular assignments, any extra reading (recommended by the lecturer or not) necessary to achieve that goal, taking outstanding notes, outlining the course (if the group so desires), being available for questions and preparing various practice tests, mid-term and final exams, as needed, to help test the other students' knowledge.

Needless to say, all of the other students attend all lectures or classes, take their own notes, do their own reading and homework assignments. But the student assigned to that course attempts to learn as much as the tutor, to actually be the 'substitute tutor' of that course in the study group. (So if you have five courses, a five-person study group is ideal.)

■ Make meeting times and assignments formal and rigorous. Consider establishing rigid rules of conduct. Better to shake out the non-serious students early. You do not want anyone who is working as little as possible but hoping to take advantage of your hard work.

■ Consider appointing a chairperson (rotating weekly, if you wish) in charge of keeping everyone on schedule and settling disputes before they disrupt the study group.

■ However you organise, clearly decide early the exact require-ments and assignments of each student. Again, you never want the feeling to emerge that one or two of you are trying to 'jump on the bandwagon' of the others.

Where should you study?

1 **At the library**. There may be numerous choices, from the large reading room, to quieter, sometimes deserted speciality rooms, to your own study cubicle.

2 **At home**. Remember that this is the place where distractions are most likely to occur. No one tends to telephone you at the library, and little brothers (or your own children) will not find you easily in there. But home is, of course, usually the most convenient place to make your study head-quarters. It may not, however, be the most effective.

3 **At a friend's, neighbour's or relative's.** This may not be an option at all for many of you, even on an occasional basis, but you still may want to set up one or two alternative study sites. Despite many experts' opinion that you must study in the same place every night, I have a friend who simply craves some variety to help motivate him. He has four different places in which he likes to study and simply rotates them from night to night. Do whatever you find works best for you.

4 **In an empty classroom.** Certainly an option at many colleges and perhaps some independent schools, it is an interesting idea mainly because so few students have ever thought of it. While not a likely option at a state school, it never hurts to ask if you can make some arrangements. Since many sports teams practise until 6pm or later, there may be a part of the school open – and usable with permission – even if the rest is locked up tight.

5 **At your job.** Whether you are a student working part time or a full-time worker going to college part time, you may be able to make arrangements to use an empty office, even during regular office hours, or perhaps after everyone has left (depending on how much your boss trusts you). If you are in secondary school and a parent, friend or relative works nearby, you may be able to work from just after school until closing time at that person's workplace,

When should you study?

As far as possible, create a routine time of day for your studying. Some experts say that doing the same thing at the same time every day is the most effective way to organise any ongoing task. Some students find it easier to set aside specific blocks of time during the day, every day, in which they plan to study.

No matter who you are, the time of day when you will study is determined by the following factors.

1 **Study when you are at your best**. When is your peak performance period – the time of day you do your best work? This period varies from person to person – you may be dead to the world until noon but able to study well into the night, or up and alert at the crack of dawn but distracted and tired if you try to burn the midnight oil.

2 **Consider your sleep habits**. Habit is a very powerful influence. If you always set your alarm for 7am, you may find that you wake up then even when you forget to set it. If you have become used to going to sleep around 11pm, you will undoubtedly become quite tired if you try to stay up studying until 2am, and probably accomplish very little in those three extra hours.

3 **Study when you can**. Although you want to sit down to study when you are mentally most alert, external factors also play a role in deciding when you study. Being at your best is a great goal but not always possible: study whenever circumstances allow.

4 **Consider the complexity of the assignment when you allocate time**. The tasks themselves may have a great effect on your schedule. Do not schedule one hour for an 80-page reading assignment when you know you read half a page a minute... on a good day.

Evaluate your study area

Whatever location you choose as your study base, how you set up your study area can affect your ability to stay focused and, if you are not careful, seriously inhibit quality study time. Sit down at your desk or study area now and evaluate your own study environment.

1 Do you have one or two special places reserved just for studying? Or do you study wherever seems convenient or available at the time?

2 Is your study area a pleasant place? Would you offer it to a friend as a good place to study? Or do you dread it because it is so depressing?

3 How is the lighting? Is it too dim or too bright? Is the whole desk well lit? Or only portions of it?

4 Are all the materials you need handy?

5 What else do you do here? Do you eat? Sleep? Write letters? Read for pleasure? If you try to study in the same place you sit to listen to your music or chat on the phone, you may find yourself doing one when you think you are doing the other.

6 Is your study area in a high-traffic or low-traffic area? How often are you interrupted by people passing by?

7 Can you close the door to the room to avoid disturbances and outside noise?

8 When do you spend the most time here? What time of day do you study? Is it when you are at your best? Or do you inevitably study when you are tired and less productive?

9 Are your files, folders and other study materials organised and near the work area? Do you have some filing system in place for them?

Staying focused on your studies

If you find yourself doodling and dawdling more than reading and remembering, try these solutions.

▮ **Create a work environment in which you are comfortable**. The size, style and placement of your desk, chair and lighting may all affect whether or not you are distracted from the work at hand. Take the time to design the area that is perfect for you.

▮ **Turn up the lights**. Experiment with the placement and intensity of lighting in your study area until you find what is best for you, both in terms of comfort and as a means of staying awake and focused.

▮ **Set some rules**. Let family, relatives and especially friends know how important your studying is and that specific hours are inviolate.

▮ **Take the breaks you need**. Do not just follow well inten-tioned but bogus advice about how long you should study before taking a break. Break when you need to.

Fighting tiredness and boredom

You have chosen the best study spot and no one could fault you on its set-up. You are still using match sticks to prop up your eyelids? Help is on the way.

▮ **Take a nap**. What a thought! When you are too tired to study, take a short nap to revive yourself. Maximise that nap's ef-fect by keeping it short – 20 minutes is ideal, 40 minutes the absolute maximum. After that, you go into another phase of sleep and you may wake even more tired than before.

▮ **Have a drink**. A little caffeine will not harm you – a cup of coffee or tea, a Coke. Just be careful not to overdo it – caffeine's 'wake-up' properties seem to reverse when you reach a certain level, making you far more tired than you were.

▮ **Turn down the heat**. Do not be cold, but too warm a room will inevitably make you doze… while your essay remains unwritten on your desk.

▮ **Shake a leg**. Go for a walk, jog around the kitchen, do a few step-ups – even mild physical exertion will give you an immediate lift.

▪ **Change your study schedule**. Presuming you have some choice here, find a way to study when you are normally more awake and/or most efficient.

Studying with young children

As many more of you are studying while raising a family, I want to give you some ideas that will help you cope with the Charge of the Preschool Light Brigade.

Plan activities to keep the children occupied

The busier you are at college and/or at work, the more time your children will want to spend with you when you are at home. If you spend some time with them, it may be easier for them to play alone, especially if you have created projects they can work on while you are working on your homework.

Make the children part of your study routine

Children love routine, so why not include them in yours? If 4pm–6pm is always 'Mum's Study Time,' they will soon get used to it, especially if you make spending other time with them a priority and if you take the time to give them something to do during those hours.

Use the television as a baby sitter

While many of you will have a problem with this it may be the lesser of two evils. You can certainly rent (or tape) enough quality films so you do not have to worry about the children watching street gangs bash skulls (or bashing skulls themselves on some video game system).

Plan your study accordingly

Unless you are a 'perfect parent', all these things will not keep your children from interrupting every now and then. While you can minimise such intrusions, it is virtually impossible to eliminate them entirely. So don't try – plan your schedule assuming them. For starters, that means taking more frequent breaks to spend five minutes with your children. They will be more likely to give you the 15 or 20 minutes at a time you need if they get periodic attention themselves.

Find help

Spouses or partners can occasionally take the children out for dinner and a film (the children will encourage you to study more if you institute this), relatives can baby sit (at their homes) on a rotating basis, playmates can be invited over (allowing you to send your child to their house the next day), you may be able to swap baby-sitting chores with other parents at school, and professional day care may be available at your child's school or in someone's home for a couple of hours a day.

Finally, use the pre-test organiser on pages 38 and 39 to work out your plan of action for the next test.

You _can_ be successful without killing yourself.

Pre-test Organiser

Lesson: _____ **Teacher:** _____

Test date: _____ **Time:** From _____ to _____

Place: _____

Special instructions to myself (eg, take calculator, dictionary, etc): _____

_____

Materials I need to study for this test/exam:

- ❏ Textbooks
- ❏ Workbook
- ❏ Lesson notes
- ❏ Handouts
- ❏ Tapes/videos
- ❏ Old exam papers
- ❏ Other _____

Format of the exam will be (multiple-choice number of questions, essays, etc, and total points for each section):

_____

_____

_____

_____

Study group meetings (times, places):

1 _____
2 _____
3 _____
4 _____
5 _____

Material to be covered:
Indicate topics, sources and amount of review (light or
heavy) required. Tick box when review is completed.

Topic   Sources   Review
_____   _____   ☐ _____
_____   _____   ☐ _____
_____   _____   ☐ _____
_____   _____   ☐ _____
_____   _____   ☐ _____
_____   _____   ☐ _____
_____   _____   ☐ _____

Ater the test:

Grade I expected _____ Grade I received _____
What did I do that helped me?

_____

_____

_____

_____

_____

What else should I have done?

_____

_____

_____

_____

_____

4 *Organise your months, weeks and days*

Now you're ready to plan!

We will begin by developing a time management plan for an entire term... before it begins, of course. This term plan will allow you to keep your sights on the 'big picture'. You will see the forest, even when you are surrounded by trees... and a majority of them are giant oaks.

By being able to see an overview of your entire term – every major assignment, every exam, every essay, every appointment – you will be less likely to get caught up spending more time on a lower priority lesson, just because it requires regular formal homework, while at the same time falling behind in a more important one, which only requires reading.

When you can actually see you have an exam in accounting the same week your zoology project is due to be handed in, you can plan ahead and finish the project early. If you decide (for whatever reason) not to do so, at least you will not be caught by surprise when the crunch comes.

Start planning early

For your long-term planning to be effective, however, you must start early. Students who fail to plan before the academic term begins often find themselves wasting time filling in their schedules one event at a time during the term. They may also find themselves feeling disorganised throughout the term. Starting early, on the other hand, increases your ability to follow a systematic plan of attack.

Most college and university students – and some sixth form students – are able to pick and choose courses according to their own schedules, likes, dislikes, goals, etc. The heartiness of such freedom should be tempered with the common-sense approach you are trying to develop through reading this book.

Here are a few hints to help you along.

1 Whenever possible, consider each lecturer's reputation as you decide whether to select a particular course (especially if it is an overview or introductory course that is offered in two or three sessions). Word soon gets around as to which lecturers' talks are stimulating and rewarding – an environment in which learning is a joy, even if it is not a subject you like.

2 Attempt to select lectures so that your schedule is balanced on a weekly and even a daily basis, although this will not always be possible or advisable. (Do not change your degree course just to fit your schedule.) Try to leave an open hour or half-hour between lectures – it is ideal for review, post-class note-taking, quick trips to the library, and so on.

3 Try to alternate challenging lectures with those that come more easily to you. Studying is a process of positive reinforcement. You will need encouragement along the way.

4 Avoid late-evening or early-morning lectures, especially if such scheduling provides you with large gaps of non-effective time.

5 Set a personal study pace and follow it. Place yourself on a study diet, the key rule of which is: do not overeat.

Identify the starting line

You cannot race off to your ultimate goal until you find out where your starting line is. So the first step necessary to overhaul your current routine is to identify that routine in detail. My suggestion is to chart, in 15-minute slots, how you spend every minute of every day. While a day or two might be sufficient for some of you, I recommend you chart your activities for an entire week, including the weekend.

This is especially important if, like many people, you have huge pockets of time that seem to disappear, but in reality are devoted to things like 'resting' after you wake up, putting on makeup or shaving, reading the paper, waiting for public transport or driving to and from school or work. Could you use an extra hour or two a day, either for studying or for fun? Make better use of such 'dead' time and you will find all the time you need.

For example, learn how to do multiple tasks at the same time. Listen to a book on tape while you are working around the house; practise vocabulary or maths tables while you are driving; ask your children, parents or roommates to test you for an approaching exam while you are washing up, vacuuming or dusting; and always carry your calendar, notebook(s), pens and a textbook with you – you can get a phenomenal amount of reading or studying done while queuing at the bank, in the library, at the supermarket or on a bus or train.

Strategy tip: Identify those items on your daily calendar, whatever their priority, that can be completed in 15 minutes or less. These are the ideal tasks to tackle at the launderette, while waiting for a librarian to locate a book you need or while queuing anywhere.

Collect what you need

As you begin your planning session, make sure you have all the information and materials you need to make a quality plan. Gather your course syllabuses, work schedule, dates of important family events, holidays or trips, other personal commitments (doctor's appointments, parties, etc); and a calendar of any extracurricular events in which you plan to participate. Keeping track of your day-to-day activities – lessons, appointments, regular daily homework assignments and daily or weekly tests – will be dealt with later in this chapter. For the moment, I want to talk about the projects – termly assignments, theses, studying for mid-term exams and finals, etc – that require completion over a long period of time – weeks, maybe even months.

Creating your project board

There are two excellent tools you can use for your long-term planning. The first is a project board, which you can put on any blank wall or right above your desk. You do not need to construct your own project board, although it is certainly the least expensive alternative. There are ready-made charts for professionals available in a variety of formats for your convenience, including magnetic and erasable. (Once again you are learning something that you can use throughout your entire life: professionals call their project boards 'flow charts'.) Your local art supplier, stationer or bookshop may have a selection of these.

How does the project board work? It is just a variation on a typical calendar. You can set it up vertically, with the months running down the left-hand side and the projects across the top. Or you can change it round and have the dates across the top and the projects running vertically (this is the way a lot of the ready-made ones are sold). It all depends on the available space you have on your wall.

Using your project board

For each project, there is a key preparatory step before you can use the chart: you have to break down each general assignment into its component parts, the specific tasks involved in any large project.

Also include on your project board time for studying for all your final exams. Cramming for exams does not work very well in the short term and does not work at all over the long term, so take my advice and make it a habit to review your class notes on each subject on a weekly or monthly basis.

As a result of this plan, you will allocate little time to last-minute cramming or even studying for a specific exam the week before it takes place (only a couple of hours to go over any details you are still a little unsure of or spend on areas you think will be on the exam). While others are burning the midnight oil in the library the night before each exam, you are getting a good night's sleep and will enter the exam refreshed, relaxed and confident. Seems like a better plan to me.

As a by-product of this study schedule, you will also find that salient facts and ideas will remain with you long after anybody is testing you on them.

Now that you have your project board, what do you do with it? Keep adding any and all other important projects throughout the term and continue to revise it according to actual time spent, as opposed to time allocated. Getting into this habit will make you more aware of how much time to allocate to future projects and make sure that the more you do so, the more accurate your estimates will be.

Using a term planning calendar

The term planning calendar, an example of which is shown on page 46, can be used in conjunction with or in place of the project board.

To use it with the project board

Start by transferring all the information from the project board to your term planning calendar. Then add your weekly lesson schedule, work schedule, family celebrations, holidays and trips, club meetings and extracurricular activities. Everything. The idea is to make sure your calendar has all your scheduling information, while your project board contains just the briefest summary that you can take in at a glance.

Leave your project board on your wall at home but carry your term calendar with you. Whenever new projects, appointments, meetings, etc are scheduled, add them immediately to your calendar. Then transfer the steps involving major projects to your project board.

To use it in place of the project board

Forget the project board. Put all the information – including the steps of all your projects and the approximate time you expect each to take – straight on to the calendar.

It is up to you which way to go. Personally, I prefer using both, for one simple reason: I like being able to look at the wall and see the entire term at a glance. I find it much easier to see how everything 'fits' together in this way rather than trying to glance at a dozen different weekly calendars or even three-monthly ones.

The fat lady isn't singing yet

It is time to become even more organised. The project board and term planning calendar have given you a good start by helping you to schedule the entire term. Now it is time to learn about the tools that will help you organise your days and weeks.

For any time management system to work, it has to be used continually. Before you go on, make an appointment with yourself for the end of the week – Sunday night is perfect – to sit down and plan for the following week. You do not have to spend a lot of time – a half-hour is probably all it will take to review your commitments for the week and schedule the necessary study time.

Despite its brevity, this may be the best time you spend all week, because you will reap the benefits of it throughout the week and beyond.

Step 1: Make your 'to do' list

First, identify everything you need to do this week.

Look at your project board and/or term planning calendar to determine what tasks need to be completed this week for all of your major projects. Add any other tasks that must be done – from sending a birthday present to your sister to attending your monthly volunteer meeting to completing homework that may have been set recently.

Once you have created your list, you can move on to the next step, putting your tasks in order of importance.

Step 2: Prioritise your tasks

When you sit down to study without a plan, you just dive into the first project that comes to mind. The problem with this approach has been discussed earlier: there is no guarantee that

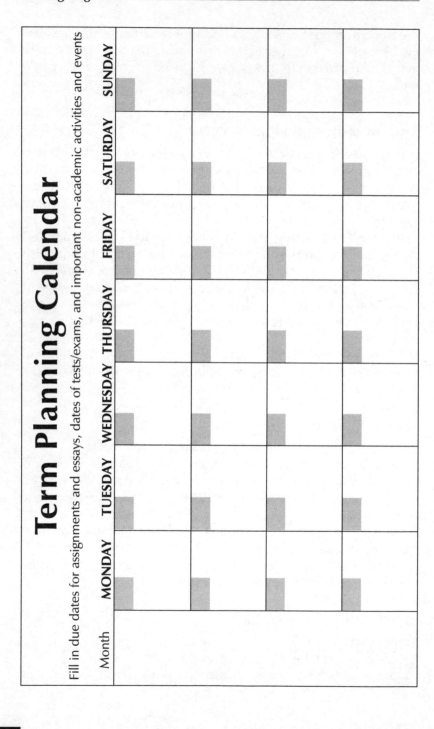

Term Planning Calendar

Fill in due dates for assignments and essays, dates of tests/exams, and important non-academic activities and events

Month	MONDAY	TUESDAY	WEDNESDAY	THURSDAY	FRIDAY	SATURDAY	SUNDAY

the first thing that comes to mind will be the most important. The point of the weekly priority task sheet is to help you arrange your tasks in order of importance. By doing this, even if you find yourself without enough time for everything, you can at least finish the most important assignments.

First, ask yourself this question, 'If I only got a few things done this week, what would I want them to be?' Mark these high-priority tasks with an 'H'. After you have identified the 'urgent' items, consider those tasks that are least important – items that could wait until the following week to be done, if necessary. (This may include tasks you consider very important but that do not have to be completed this week.) These are low-priority items, at least for this week – mark them with an 'L'.

All the other items fit somewhere between the critical tasks and the low-priority ones. Review the remaining items. If you are sure none of them are either 'H' or 'L', mark them with an 'M', for middle priority.

Strategy tip: If you push aside the same low-priority item day after day, week after week, at some point you should stop and decide whether it is something you need to do at all. This is a strategic way to make a task or problem 'disappear'. In the business world, some managers purposefully avoid confronting a number of problems, waiting to see if they will simply solve themselves through benign neglect. If it works in business, it can work in school and college.

A completed priority task sheet is on page 51. A blank form you can photocopy is on page 53.

Step 3: Fill in your daily schedule

Before you start adding essays, projects, homework, study time, etc, to your calendar, fill in the 'knowns' – the time you need to sleep, eat, work and attend class. Even if your current routine consists of meals on the run and sleep whenever you find it, build the assumption into your schedule that you are going to get eight hours of sleep and three decent meals a day. You may surprise yourself and find that there is still enough time to do everything you need. (Although all of us probably know someone who sleeps three hours a night, eats only junk and still finds a way to get nothing but As, most experts would argue that regular, healthy eating and a decent sleep schedule are key attributes to any successful study system.)

Now you are ready to transfer the items on your priority task sheet to your daily schedule forms. (See page 52 for a completed example of a daily schedule, page 54 for a blank form you can photocopy.)

Put in the 'H' items first, followed by the 'M' items. Then, fit in as many of the 'L' items that you still have room for. By following this procedure, you will ensure you give the amount of time needed for your most important priorities. You can schedule your most productive study time for your most important tasks, and slot in your lower priorities as they fit.

Your three-hour block of free time on Wednesday afternoon? Schedule your 'H' priority research gathering, and plan to start that psychology assignment, an 'L' priority, between lunch and your 2pm class on Thursday.

Other considerations

Besides the importance of the task and the available time you have to complete it, other factors will determine how you fit your daily schedules together. Some factors will be beyond your control – work schedules, appointments with lecturers, personal tutors, doctors. But there are plenty of factors you do control and should consider as you put together your daily schedules each week.

Schedule enough time for each task – time to 'warm up' and get the task accomplished, but, particularly when working on long-term projects, not so much time that you 'burn out'. Every individual is different, but most students study best for blocks of one and a half to three hours, depending on the subject.

Do not overdo it. Plan your study time in blocks, breaking up work time with short leisure activities. (It is helpful to add these to your schedule as well.) For example, you have set aside three hours on Wednesday afternoon for that research assignment. Plan a 15-minute walk to the cafeteria somewhere in the middle of that study block. You will find that these breaks help you to think more clearly and creatively when you get back to studying.

Even if you tend to like longer blocks of study time, be careful about scheduling study 'marathons' – a six- or eight-hour stretch rather than a series of two-hour sessions. The longer the period you schedule, the more likely you will have to fight the demons of procrastination. By convincing yourself that you are really studying flat out, you will also find it easier to justify time-wasting distractions, scheduling longer breaks and, before long, quitting before you should.

Use your daily schedule daily

Each night (or in the morning before the day really begins) look at your schedule for the forthcoming day. How much free time is there? Are there 'surprise' tasks that are not on your schedule but need to be? Are there conflicts you were unaware of at the beginning of the week?

If you plan well at the beginning of the week, this should not happen often, but it invariably does. Sometimes you will discover a lesson is cancelled or a meeting postponed, which leaves you with a schedule change. By checking your daily schedule daily – either the night before or first thing in the morning – you will be able to respond to these changes.

How do you know whether to enter an assignment on your daily schedule or put it on the project board first?

If it is a simple task and if it will definitely be accomplished within a week – study for a classroom test, read a couple of chapters for your English literature lesson – put it on the appropriate daily schedule sheet(s).

However, if it is a task that is complicated – requiring further breakdown into specific steps and/or one that will require more than a week to complete, it should be 'flow charted' on your project board. Then the individual steps should be added to your daily schedules. (I like to plan everything out the night before. It is a fantastic feeling to wake up and start the day completely organised.)

The most important 15 minutes of your day

Set aside 15 minutes every day to go over your daily and weekly priorities. While many business people like to make this the first 15 minutes of their day, I recommend making it the last 15 minutes of your day. Why? Three good reasons.

1 **Your ideas will be fresher**. It is easier to analyse at the end of the day what you have accomplished... and have not.

2 **It is a good way to end the day**. Even if your 'study day' ends at 11pm, you will feel fully prepared for the next day and ready to relax, anxiety free.

3 **You will get off to a good start the next morning**. If you use the morning to plan, it is easy to turn a 15-minute planning session into an hour of aimless 'thinking'. While others are fumbling for a cup of coffee, you are off and running.

Priority Rating	Scheduled?	**Priority Tasks This Week** Week beginning **28/3** and ending **3/4**
		Biology Essay
H		*– Library Search*
M		*– Outline*
L		*– Rough Draft*
		Chemistry Assignments
H		*– Ch 4*
M		*– Ch 5*
M		*– Revise for test*

Daily Schedule

date: **28/3**

Assignments Due

Bio Lab work
Maths Ch 4

To Do/Errands

Call Eric – 871-4031
Books to library
 – Bank
 – Supermarket
Stop in at Rob's for
book

Homework

1. Maths Ch 5, 1-9
2. Biology Essay
   (rough draft)

Schedule

5
6
7
8
9 Biology
10 Chemistry
11
12 Lunch w/ Kate
1 Read Ch 5 (Chem)
2
3 Maths lesson
4 TRAVEL
5
6 Maths homework
7 Work on essay
8 ←
9
10
11
12

Priority Rating	Scheduled?	**Priority Tasks This Week** Week beginning ▢ and ending ▢

Daily Schedule

date:

Assignments Due

To Do/Errands

Homework

Schedule

5
6
7
8
9
10
11
12
1
2
3
4
5
6
7
8
9
10
11
12

5 *Dealing with life's daily traumas*

Your organisational plan should be simple. Why agree to do another complicated project that demands your time and mental energies? No matter how basic and easy to use your programme may be, this does not guarantee that you will not be plagued with a time management problem from time to time.

As you try to implement these skills in your life, you are bound to have some slip-ups. Learn some problem-solving skills so these study roadblocks do not stop your progress completely.

If you run into a 'wall' on your path to organisational success, the best solution is to find creative ways to get around it, rather than trying to crash your way through it.

Time flies when you are having fun...

And sometimes even when you are not. No matter how hard you try to stick to your schedule, you find your assignments always take a lot longer than planned.

You schedule an hour to do your economics homework, and it takes you twice that long. You plan an afternoon at the library for research, and it is closing time before you are ready to leave. It seems you spend all your time studying – and you are still not getting it done.

Solutions: It is time for an attitude check. Are you being too much of a perfectionist? Is it taking you so long to read because you are trying to memorise every word? Make sure your expectations for yourself are realistic. Do not exaggerate the importance of lower priority assignments.

Consider altering your behaviour – with a little help from an alarm clock. If you have planned an hour for your reading assignment, set the clock to go off when you should have completed it. Then, stop reading and go on to the next task. If you have not finished, reassure yourself that you can go back to it later. You will probably become conditioned to complete your assignments more quickly, and you will not run the risk of leaving your other, perhaps more important, work unfinished.

'I'm allergic to my desk'

There is nothing wrong with your study area. It is in a quiet corner of the house with few distractions. All your materials are nearby, and the area is well lit and well ventilated. But... every time you sit down to study, you find yourself coming up with any excuse to leave. Unable to focus on any assignment, your mind wanders off.

Solution: It can happen. You set up the ideal study area, follow your time management system and stick to your schedule religiously. Your intentions are good, but, for some reason, it does not work. Bad vibes, maybe. What can you do?

Change your environment.

Just as you can condition yourself to study, you can also condition yourself not to study in a particular location. Stick to your schedule, but try another area – another floor in the library, or even a place that may not seem to be as conducive to quiet study. Maybe you are one of those people who needs a little music or activity in the background to concentrate.

If changing your environment does not help, consider altering your study routine. Are you trying to study at a time of day when you have far too much pent-up energy? Maybe changing your study time to an earlier or later time would help. Try taking a brisk walk or exercising before you begin studying.

Think about other behaviour: have you had several cups of coffee (or cans of Coke) prior to your study period? Caffeine overdose – or too much sugar and caffeine – can make it very difficult to concentrate.

A conspiracy to keep you from studying

Friends and family visit or phone when you are studying because they know that is the best time to find you at home.

Or you are interrupted by phone calls for family members or roommates. Worse yet are the calls from people taking surveys, asking for donations or trying to sell you something.

Solutions: A ringing phone is virtually impossible to ignore. Even if you are determined not to pick it up, it still demands your attention. An answering-machine will eliminate involvement in lengthy conversations, but your train of thought will still be interrupted.

There are a few environment–altering solutions: turn off the ringer or unplug the phone and let your answering-machine take the calls while you are studying. Or remove yourself from within hearing distance – go to the library.

A little help from your 'friends'

Your roommate, whose study hours differ from yours, always seems to want to spend 'quality bonding time' in the middle of your heavy reading assignments.

Solutions: It is not rude to refuse to talk to someone while you are studying, but it often feels like that, and I would rather feel guilty about not studying than being rude to a friend. A favourite tip from human relations specialists is to respond in a positive but diverting way – eg, 'It sounds like this is important to you. I really want to hear more. Can we talk in an hour when I have finished this, so I can concentrate more on your problem?' (Agreed, your roommate would look at you as if you were mad if you talked like this. Put it in your own words – it is the attitude that is important.)

Another solution might be to put up a 'Do Not Disturb' sign, indicating the time you will be available to talk. The visual signal helps remind others that you are busy before they unintentionally interrupt you with small talk.

You can't count on anyone

You painstakingly plan your schedule each week, religiously keeping track of each appointment, assignment and commitment you have. Unfortunately, others do not seem to have the same sense of responsibility as you do. Your friends cancel social engagements, you arrive on time for a meeting and no one else in the group shows up, even your teacher postpones the pre-exam study session.

Solution: Yes, it is time for another attitude adjustment. Welcome to the real world.

First of all, there is really nothing you can do when someone else cancels or postpones a scheduled appointment. But if you remember, in the very first chapter of this book I said that fanaticism is not an element of a good time management programme.

Occasional – and sometimes more than occasional – cancellations, postponements or reschedulings should not ruin your schedule.

Try looking at such last-minute changes as opportunities. Your tutor cancelled your appointment? That means a free hour to get ahead in calculus, read your history, work out at the gym… or just do nothing.

Old habits die hard

As you begin to implement your own organisational system for success, you may need to rid yourself of some old habits.

1 **Do not make your schedule too vague**. When you are scheduling your time, be specific about which tasks you plan to do, and when you plan to do them.

2 **Do not delay your planning**. It is easy to convince yourself that you will plan the details of a particular task when the time comes. But this makes it much too easy to forget your homework when your friends invite you to go to the park or out for a snack.

3 **Write everything down**. Not having to remember all these items will free up space in your brain for the things you need to concentrate on or do have to remember. As a general rule, write down the so-called little things and you will avoid data overload and clutter.

4 **Learn to manage distractions**. 'Don't respond to the urgent and forget the important.' It is easy to become distracted when the phone rings, your baby brother chooses to trash your room or you realise your favourite TV programme is coming on. But do not just drop your books and run off. Take a few seconds to make sure you have reached a logical stopping point.

5 **Do not 'shotgun' plan**. Even if you have not been following a systematic time management approach, you may have had some way of keeping important dates and events in mind. Some students use what might be called the 'shotgun' approach – writing down assignments, dates and times on whatever is available. They end up with so many slips of paper in so many places, their planning attempts are virtually worthless.

   Record all future events and tasks on your project board and/or term planning calendar. Always have your calendar with you so you can refer to it when you are planning a specific week or day or need to add an appointment or assignment to it.

6 **Do not 'over schedule'**. As you begin to follow a time management programme, you may find yourself trying to schedule too much of your time. Once you get the 'effectiveness bug' and become aware of how much you can accomplish, it might be tempting to squeeze more and more into your life.

7 **Be honest with yourself** when determining those things that require more effort, those that come easier to you. Chances are you cannot complete the outline for your project assignment, study three chapters of biology and do your French assignment in the two hours you have between lessons and work. Schedule enough time to complete each assignment. Whenever possible, schedule pleasurable activities after study time, not before. They will act as incentives, not distractions.

8 **Remember that time is relative**. Car trips take longer if you have to schedule frequent stops for petrol, food, necessities, etc, longer still if you start out during rush hour. Similarly, libraries are more crowded at certain times of the day or year, which will affect how fast you can get books you need, etc. So take the time of day into account.

9 **Be prepared**. As assignments are entered on your calendar, make sure you also enter items needed for their completion – texts, other books you have to buy, borrow or get from the library, special materials, etc. There is nothing worse than sitting down to do that assignment you have put off until the last minute and realising that though you are finally ready to get to work, your supplies are not... and at 10pm, you do not have a lot of options.

10 **Be realistic**. Plan according to your schedule, your goals and your aptitudes, not some ephemeral 'standard'. Allocate the time you expect a project to take you, not the time it might take someone else, how long your teacher tells you it should take, etc.

11 **Be flexible, monitor and adjust**. No calendar is an island. Any new assignment will affect whatever you have already scheduled. If you have a reasonably light schedule when a new assignment suddenly appears, it can be slotted into your calendar and finished as scheduled. But if you have already planned virtually every hour for the next two weeks, any addition may force you to change a whole day's plan. Be flexible and be ready. It will happen.

12 **Look for more time savings**. If you find that you are consistently allotting more time than necessary to a specific chore – giving yourself one hour to review your English notes every Sunday but always finishing in 45 minutes or less – change your future schedule accordingly.

13 **Accomplish one task before going on to the next one** – do not skip around.

14 **Do your least favourite chores** (study assignments, projects, whatever) first – you will feel better getting them out of the way.

15 **Try anything that works.** You may decide that colour coding your calendar – red for assignments that must be accomplished that week, blue for steps in longer-term projects (which give you more flexibility), yellow for personal time and appointments, green for lessons, etc – makes it easier for you to tell at a glance what you need to do and when you need to do it.

16 **Adapt these tools to your own use**. Try anything you think may work – use it if it does, discard it if it does not.

There are thinkers and there are doers.

And there are those who think a lot about doing.

Organising your life requires you to actually use the project board, term calendar, priority task sheets and daily schedules we have discussed, not just waste more time 'planning' instead of studying.

Planning is an ongoing learning process. Dive in and plan for your next academic term. Or if you are currently in the middle of a term, plan the remainder of it now. As you use your plan in the forthcoming weeks and months, you will come up with new ideas for improving your time management system in the future and tailoring it to your own needs.

6 Get organised for the classroom

The pitfalls of poor note-taking skills

Most students take too many notes or too few.

Many of you will develop severe cramp in an effort to reproduce every single word your teachers utter.

Others take notes so sparse that when reviewed weeks – or hours – later, they will make so little sense that they might as well have been hieroglyphics.

If you feel compelled to take down your teacher's every word, or recopy your entire text, you certainly will not have much of a social life – where would you find the time? Maybe you are so horrified at the prospect of reliving those hours of lectures and chapters of text that you simply never review your notes. And if you skip note-taking altogether... well, I do not need to tell you what kind of marks you should expect.

Take notes only on the material that helps you develop a thorough understanding of your subject... and get good marks. You should do it in a way that is, first and foremost, useful and understandable to you. A method that is easy to use would be a real plus.

Most students have a difficult time developing a good note-taking technique and recognising the information that always shows up on exams – an understanding of which is essential for good results.

Failing to learn good note-taking methods, they resort to what I think are useless substitutes, such as tape recorders and photocopying machines.

Know your teacher

First and foremost, you must know and understand the kind of teacher you have and his or her likes, dislikes, preferences, style and what he or she expects you to get out of the course.

Depending on your analysis of your teacher's habits, goals and tendencies, preparation may vary quite a bit, whatever the chosen format.

Take something as simple as asking questions during lessons, which I encourage you to do whenever you do not understand a key point. Some teachers are very confident fielding questions at any time during a lesson; others prefer questions to be held until the end of the day's lesson; still others discourage questions (or any interaction for that matter) entirely. Learn when and how your teacher likes to field questions and ask them accordingly.

No matter how ready a classroom group is to enter into a free-wheeling discussion, some teachers fear losing control and veering away from their very specific lesson plan. Such teachers may well encourage discussion but always try to steer it into a predetermined path (their lesson plan). Other teachers thrive on chaos, in which case you can never be sure what is going to happen.

Approaching a lesson with the former teacher should lead you to participate as much as possible in the classroom discussion, but warn you to stay within whatever boundaries he or she has obviously set.

Getting ready for a lesson taught by the latter kind of teacher requires much more than just reading the text – there will be a lot of emphasis on your understanding key concepts, interpretation, analysis and your ability to apply those lessons to cases never mentioned in your text at all.

In general, here is how you should plan to prepare for any lesson before you walk through the door and take your seat.

Complete all assignments

Regardless of a particular teacher's style or the classroom format he or she is using, virtually every course you take will have a formal text (or two or three or more) assigned to it. Although the way the text explains or covers particular topics may differ substantially from your teacher's approach to the same material, your text is still the basis of the course and a key ingredient in your studying. You must read it, plus any other assigned books, before arriving at the lesson.

You may sometimes feel you can get away without reading assigned books beforehand, especially in a lecture format where you know the chance of being called on is fairly slim. But fear of being questioned on the material is certainly not the only reason for reading the material that has been assigned. You will be lost if the lecturer decides – for the first time ever – to spend the entire period asking the students questions. I have seen this happen and it is not pleasant for the unprepared.

You will also find it harder to take clear and concise notes because you will not know what is in the text (and you will be frantically taking notes on material you could have underlined in your books the night before) or be able to evaluate the relative importance of the teacher's remarks.

Remember: completing your reading assignment includes not just reading the main text but any other books or articles previously assigned, plus handouts that may have been previously given out. It also means completing any non-reading assignments – handing in a lab report, preparing a list of topics or being ready to present your oral report.

Review your notes

Both from your reading and from the previous lecture. Your teacher is probably going to start this lecture or discussion from the point he or she left off last time and you probably will not remember where that point was from week to week, unless you check your notes.

Have questions ready

Go over your questions before the lecture. This will let you tick off the ones the lecturer or teacher answers along the way and you will only ask those left unanswered.

Prepare required materials

Include your notebook, text, pens or pencils and other such basics, plus particular classroom requirements like a calculator, drawing paper or other books.

Learn 'selective' listening

Taking concise, clear notes is first and foremost the practice of discrimination – developing your ability to separate the essential from the superfluous, key concepts, key facts, key ideas from all the rest. In turn, this requires the ability to listen to what your teacher is saying and copying down only what you need so as to understand the concept. For some, that could mean a single sentence. For others, a detailed example will be the key.

Remember: the quality of your notes usually has little to do with their length – three key lines that reveal the core concepts of a whole lecture are far more valuable than paragraphs of less important data.

So why do some people keep trying to take verbatim notes, convinced that the more pages they cover with scribbles the better students they are being? It is probably a sign of insecurity – they have not read the material and/or do not have a clue about what is being discussed, but at least they will have complete notes.

Even if you find yourself wandering helplessly in the lecturer's wake, so unsure of what she is saying that you cannot begin to separate the important, noteworthy material from the non-essential verbiage, use the techniques discussed in this book to organise and condense your notes anyway.

If you really find yourself so lost that you are just wasting your time, consider adding a review session to your schedule (to read or reread the appropriate text) and, if the lecture or lesson is available again at another time, attend again. Yes it is, strictly speaking, a waste of your precious study time, but not if it is the only way to learn and understand important material.

Take notes on what you don't know

You know the first lines of Macbeth. You know the chemical formula for water. You know when the Great Fire of London started. So why waste time and space writing them down?

Frequently, your teachers will present material you already know in order to set the stage for further discussion or to introduce material that is new or more difficult. Do not be so conditioned to automatically copy down dates, vocabulary, terms, formulas and names that you mindlessly take notes on information you already know. You will just be wasting your time – both in the lecture and later, when you review your over-detailed notes.

This is why some experts recommend that you bring your notes or outline of your textbook reading to the lesson and add your lesson notes to them. I think it is an effective way to easily organise all your notes for that lesson, even if it does kill the idea of highlighting or underlining your text.

Observe your teacher's style

All effective teachers develop a plan of attack for each class. They decide what points they will make, how much time they will spend reviewing assignments and previous lessons, what texts they will refer to, what anecdotes they will bring into the lecture to provide comic relief or human interest and how much time they will allow for questions.

Building a note-taking strategy around each teacher's typical plan of attack for lectures is another key to academic success.

Throughout my school days, I had to struggle to get good marks. I took copious notes, studied them every night and pored over them before every test and exam. I was rewarded for my efforts with straight As, but resented the hours I had to put in while my less ambitious friends found more intriguing ways to spend their time.

But some of the brighter students had leisure time, too. When I asked them how they did it, they shrugged their shoulders and said they did not know.

These students had an innate talent that they could not explain, a sixth sense about what to study, what were the most important things a teacher said and what teachers were most likely to ask about in exams.

In fact, when I was in a study group with some of these students, they would say, 'Don't worry, she will never ask about that.' And sure enough, she never did.

What is more, these students had forgotten many of the details I was struggling with. They had not even bothered to write any of them down, let alone try to remember them.

What these students innately knew was that items discussed during any lesson could be grouped into several categories, which varied in importance.

I Information not contained in the lesson texts and other assigned readings.

I Explanations of obscure material covered in the texts and readings but with which students might have difficulty.

I Demonstrations or examples that provided greater understanding of the subject matter.

I Background information that put the course material in context.

As you are listening to a lecturer, decide which of these categories best fits the information being presented to you. This will help you determine how detailed your notes on the material should be. (This will become easier as time passes and you get to know the lecturer.)

Read, read, read

Most good lecturers will follow a text they have selected for the course. Similarly, unless they have written the textbook themselves, most teachers will supplement it with additional information. Good teachers will look for shortcomings in textbooks and spend varying amounts of classroom time filling in these gaps.

As a result, it makes sense to stay one step ahead of your teachers. Read ahead in your textbook so that, as a teacher is speaking, you know what part of the lesson you should write down and what parts of it are already written down in your textbook. Conversely, you will immediately recognise the supplementary material on which you might need to take more detailed notes.

Will you be asked about this supplementary material in your exams?

If you ask your teacher that question, he will probably say something like, 'You are expected to know everything that is mentioned on this course.' That is why it is best to pay attention (and not ask stupid questions you already know the answers to).

You will quickly learn to tell from a teacher's body language what he considers important and what he considers superficial.

In addition, your experience with the teacher's exams and spot tests will give you a great deal of insight into what he or she considers most important.

Sit near the front of the room

Minimise distractions by sitting as close to the teacher as you can.

The farther you sit from the teacher, the more difficult it is to listen. Sitting toward the back of the room means more heads bobbing around in front of you, more students staring out of the window – encouraging you to do the same.

Sitting at the front has several benefits. You will make a terrific first impression on the teacher – you might very well be the only student sitting in the front row. He will see immediately that you have come to listen and learn, not just to take up space.

You will be able to hear the teacher's voice, and the teacher will be able to hear you when you ask and answer questions.

Finally, being able to see the teacher clearly will help ensure that your eyes do not wander around the room and out of the windows, taking your brain with them.

So, if you have the option of picking your desk in the classroom, sit at the front.

Avoid distracting classmates

The crisp eater. The doodler. The practical joker. The whisperer. Even the perfume sprayer. Your classmates may be wonderful friends, entertaining lunch companions and ultimate weekend party animals, but their quirks, idiosyncrasies and personal hygiene habits can prove distracting when you sit next to them in the classroom.

Knuckle-cracking, giggling, whispering and note-passing are just some of the evils that can divert your attention in the middle of your maths teacher's discourse on quadratic equations. Avoid them.

Listen for verbal clues

Identifying noteworthy material means finding a way to separate the wheat – that which you should write down – from the chaff – that which you should ignore. How do you do that? By listening for verbal clues and watching for the non-verbal ones.

Certainly not all teachers will give you the clues you are seeking. But many will invariably signal important material in the way they present it – pausing (waiting for all the pens to rise), repeating the same point (perhaps even one already made and repeated in your textbook), slowing down their normally supersonic lecture speed, speaking more loudly (or more softly), even by simply stating, 'I think the following is important.'

There are also numerous words and phrases that should signal noteworthy material (and, at the same time, give you the clues you need to logically organise your notes): 'First of all', 'Most importantly', 'Therefore', 'As a result', 'To summarise', 'On the other hand', 'On the contrary', 'The following (number of) reasons (causes, effects, decisions, facts, etc)'.

Such words and phrases give you the clues not only to write down the material that follows, but also to put it in context – to make a list ('First', 'The following reasons'); to establish a cause-and-effect relationship ('Therefore', 'As a result'); to establish opposites or alternatives ('On the other hand', 'On the contrary'); to signify a conclusion ('To summarise', 'Therefore'); or to offer an explanation or definition.

Look for non-verbal clues

If the teacher begins looking at the window, or his eyes glaze over, he is sending you a clear signal: 'Put your pen down. This is not going to be in the exam'. (So do not take notes.)

On the other hand, if she turns to write something on the blackboard, makes eye contact with several students and/or gestures dramatically, she is sending a clear signal about the importance of the point she is making.

Learn how to be a detective – do not overlook the clues.

Ask questions often

Being an active listener means asking yourself if you understand everything that has been discussed. If the answer is 'no', you must ask the teacher questions at an appropriate time or write down the questions you need answered later in order to understand the subject fully.

To tape or not to tape

I am opposed to using a tape recorder in the classroom as a substitute for an active brain for the following reasons.

- **It is time consuming**. To be cynical, not only will you have to waste time sitting through the lesson, you will have to waste more time listening to that lesson again.

- **It is virtually useless for review**. Fast-forwarding and rewinding cassettes to find the salient points of a lecture is torture. During the hectic days before an exam, do you really want to waste time listening to a whole lecture when you could just reread your notes?

- **It offers no backup**. Only the most diligent students record and take notes. What happens if your tape recorder malfunctions? How useful will blank or distorted tapes be when it is review time?

- **It costs money**. Compare the price of blank paper and a pen to that of a recorder, batteries and tapes. The cost of batteries alone should convince you that you are better off going on the low-tech route.

∎ **You miss the 'live' clues** we discussed earlier. When all you have is a tape, you do not see that flash in your teacher's eyes, passionate arm-flailing, stern set of the jaw, any and all of which scream, 'Pay attention, this will be in your exam'.

Create your own shorthand

You do not have to be a master of shorthand to streamline your note-taking. Here are five ways.

1 Eliminate vowels. As a sign that was everywhere in the underground used to proclaim, 'If u cn rd ths, u cn gt a gd jb'. (If you can read this, you can get a good job.) And, we might add, 'u cn b a btr stdnt'.

2 Use word beginnings ('rep' for representative) and other easy-to-remember abbreviations (ac for account).

3 Stop putting full stops after all abbreviations (they add up).

4 Create your own symbols and abbreviations based on your needs and comfort level.

 There are two specific symbols you may want to create – they will be needed again and again:

(W) That is my symbol for 'What?' as in 'What does that mean?' 'What did she say?' or 'What happened? I am completely lost'. It denotes something that has been missed – leave space in your notes to fill in the missing part of the puzzle after the lesson.

(M) That is my symbol for 'My thought'. I want to separate my thoughts during a lecture from the lecturer's – put down too many of your own ideas (without noting they are yours) and your notes begin to lose serious value.

 Feel free to use your own code for these two instances; you certainly do not have to use mine.

5 Use standard symbols in place of words. The following list may help you. You may also recognise some of these from maths and logic:

≈	Approximately
w/	With
w/o	Without
wh/	Which
→	Resulting in
←	As a result of/consequence of
+	And or also
*	Most importantly
cf	Compare; in comparison; in relation to
ff	Following
<	Less than
>	More than
=	The same as
↑	Increasing
↓	Decreasing
esp	Especially
Δ	Change
⊂	It follows that
∴	Therefore
∵	Because

While I recommend using all the 'common' symbols and abbreviations listed previously all the time, in every lesson, in order to maintain consistency, you may want to create specific symbols or abbreviations for each course. In chemistry, 'TD' may stand for thermodynamics, 'K' for the Kinetic Theory of Gases (do not mix it up with the 'K' for Kelvin). In history, 'WC' is Winston Churchill, 'PM' is the Prime Minister, 'FR' could be French Revolution (or 'freedom rider'), 'IR' is the Industrial Revolution.

How do you keep everything straight? Create a list on the first page of that course's notebook or binder section for the abbreviations and symbols you intend to use regularly throughout the term.

Expanding on your 'shorthand'

Continue to abbreviate more as additional terms become readily recognisable – in that way, the speed and effectiveness of your note-taking will increase as the academic year grinds on.

Many students are prone to write big when they are writing fast and to use only a portion of the width of their paper. They think that turning over pages quickly means they are taking good notes. All it really means is that they are taking notes that will be difficult to read or use when it is review time.

Force yourself to write small and neatly, taking advantage of the entire width of your note paper. The less unnecessary movement the better.

What to do after class

As soon as possible after your lesson, review your notes, fill in the 'blanks', mark down questions you need to research in your text or ask during the next lesson, and remember to mark any new assignments on your weekly calendar.

I tend to discourage recopying notes as a general rule, as I believe its more important to work on taking good notes the first time around and not waste the time it takes to recopy. But if you tend to write fast and illegibly, it might also be a good time to rewrite your notes so they are readable, taking the opportunity to summarise as you go. The better your notes, the better your chance of capturing and recalling the pertinent material.

The next tip is not easy for most secondary school students, but in college and university, where you have a greater say in scheduling your courses, I recommend 'one period on, one off' – a free period, even a half-hour, after each lecture to review that lecture's notes and prepare for the next one.

If you find yourself unable to take full advantage of such in-between time, schedule as little time between lessons as you can.

Are you among the missing?

Even if you diligently apply all of the tips in this chapter, it will all be in vain if you regularly miss lessons. So don't. It is especially important to attend all the lessons near the end of term. Teachers sometimes use the last week to review the entire term (what a wonderful way to minimise your own review time), and/or clarify specific topics he feels might still be fuzzy and/or answer questions. Students invariably ask about the final exam during this period, and some teachers virtually outline what is going to be on the paper.

If you must miss a lesson, find that verbatim note-taker who has not followed my advice and borrow her notes. Doing this will give you the opportunity to decide what is important enough to copy down. (Some lecturers might even lend you their notes. It is worth asking.)

7 *Organise your reading and writing*

Taking *effective* notes from your texts should:

▌ *Help you recognise* the most important points of a text.

▌ *Make it easier* for you to understand those important points.

▌ Enhance your memory of the text.

▌ Provide a *highly efficient* way to study for your exams.

Go for the gold, ignore the pyrite

Step one in effective note-taking from texts is to write down the principle points the author is trying to make. These main ideas should be placed either in the left-hand margin of your note paper, or as headings. Do not write complete sentences.

Then, write down the most important details or examples the author uses to support each of these arguments. These details should be noted under their appropriate main idea. I suggest indenting them and writing each idea on a new line, one under the other. Again, do not use complete sentences. Include only enough details so that your notes are not meaningless when you review them.

I am sure it is abundantly clear to all of you that not many best-selling authors moonlight writing textbooks. Some of the books given to you for your courses – even the ones for literature courses – are poorly written, badly organised cures for sleepless nights. Dull is the kindest word to describe all but a few of them.

Having said that, it is also clear that no matter how dull the prose, your job is to find the important details from your textbooks so that you attain good marks. To prevent you from having to wade through page after page more than once, why not take good notes the first time you read?

You can use many of the strategies you implement for taking notes in lessons for your reading assignments. Just as you use your active brain to listen carefully to what your teacher talks about, you can use that same piece of equipment to read actively:

▮ Read, then write.

▮ Make sure you understand the big picture.

▮ Take notes on what you do not know.

These same principles that we discussed in conjunction with taking notes during lessons apply to taking notes on your reading materials. But there are some additional strategies you should also consider.

Change the way you read

When we read books for pleasure, we tend to read, naturally, from the beginning to the end. (Though some of us may be guilty of taking a peep at the last chapter of a gripping mystery novel.) Yet this linear approach, beginning at point A and moving in a direct manner to point B, is not necessarily the most effective way to read texts for information.

If you find yourself ploughing diligently through your texts without having the faintest idea what you have read, it is time to change the way you read. The best students do not wade through each chapter of their textbooks from beginning to end. Instead, they read in an almost circular fashion. This is how to do it.

Look for clues

If we are curled up with the latest Stephen King thriller, we fully expect some clues along the way that will hint at the gory horror to come. We count on Agatha Christie to subtly sprinkle keys to her mysteries' solutions long before they are resolved in the drawing room.

However, most of you have probably never tried to solve the mysteries of your own textbooks by using the tell-tale signs and signals almost all of them contain. Yes, textbooks are riddled with clues that will reveal to the perceptive student all the noteworthy material that must be captured. This is how you will find them.

Chapter heads and subheads

Bold-faced headings and subheadings announce the detail about the main topic. And, in some textbooks, paragraph headings or bold-faced lead-ins announce that the author is about to provide finer details. So begin each reading assignment by going through the chapter, beginning to end, reading only the bold-faced heads and subheads.

Knowing what the author is driving at in a textbook will help you look for the important building blocks for her conclusions while you are reading. While it may not be as much fun to read a mystery novel in this way, when it comes to textbook reading and note-taking, it will make you a much more active reader, and, consequently, make it much less likely that you will doze off while reading the often heavy prose.

Pictures, graphs and charts

Most textbooks, particularly those in the sciences, will have charts, graphs, numerical tables, maps and other illustrations. All too many students see these as mere fillers – padding to glance at, then forget.

If you are giving these charts and graphs short shrift, you are really shortchanging yourself. You do not have to redraw the tables in your notes, but observe how they supplement the text and what points they emphasise, and make note of these. This will help you put them into your own words, which will help you remember them later. Also, it will ensure that you do not have to continually refer to your textbooks when revising for an exam.

Highlighted terms, vocabulary and other facts

In some textbooks, you will discover that key terms and other such information are highlighted within the body text. (And I do not mean by a previous student; consider such yellow-swathed passages with caution – their value is directly proportional to that student's final mark, which you do not know.) Whether boldface, italic, 'bulleted' or boxed, this is usually an indication that the material is noteworthy.

Questions

Some textbook publishers use a format in which key points are emphasised by questions, either within the body of the text or at the end of the chapter. If you read these questions before reading the chapter, you will have a better idea of what material you need to pay closer attention to.

These standard organisational tools should make your reading job simpler. The next time you have to read a history, geography or similar text, try skimming the assigned pages straight through. Read the heads, the subheads and the 'bullet points'. Read the first sentence of each paragraph. Then go back and start reading the details.

To summarise the skimming process:

1 Read and make sure you understand the title or heading. Try rephrasing it as a question for further clarification of what you will read.

2 Examine all the subheadings, illustrations and graphics – these will help you identify the significant matter within the text.

3 Read thoroughly the introductory paragraphs, the summary and any questions at the end of the chapter.

4 Read the first sentence of every paragraph – this generally includes the main idea.

5 Evaluate what you have gained from this process: can you answer the questions at the end of the chapter? Can you intelligently participate in a class discussion of the material?

6 Write a brief summary that encapsulates what you have learned from your skimming.

7 Based on this evaluation, decide whether a more thorough reading is required.

Now for the fine print

Now that you have a good overview of the contents by reading the heads and subheads, reviewing the summary, picking up on the highlighted words and information and considering the review questions that may be included, you are finally ready to read the chapter.

If a more thorough reading is then required, turn back to the beginning. Read one section (chapter, etc) at a time, and do not go on to the next until you have completed the following exercise.

1 Write definitions of any key terms you feel are essential to understanding the topic.

2 Write questions and answers you feel clarify the topic.

3 Write any questions for which you do not have answers – then make sure you find them through rereading, further research or asking another student or your teacher.

4 Even if you still have unanswered questions, move on to the next section and complete numbers one to three for that section. (And so on, until your reading assignment is complete.)

See if this method helps you to get a better idea on any assignment right from the start. As you did a preliminary review first, you will find that your reading will go much faster.

But... do not assume that now you can speed through your reading assignment. Do not rush through your textbook, or you will have to read it again.

Yes, we have all heard about the geniuses who can dash through 1,000 or even 2,000 words per minute and retain everything, but most of us never will read that fast. That is fine – it is better to read something slowly and remember it than rush it into oblivion. Many brilliant students – even those in law school or taking umpteen courses on the 19th-century novel – never achieve reading speeds even close to 1,000 words per minute. Some of them have to read passages they do not understand again and again to get the point. There is nothing wrong with that.

The most intelligent way to read is with comprehension, not speed, as your primary goal.

Many students underline in their textbooks or use magic markers to 'highlight' them. This is a definite sign of masochism, as it guarantees only one thing: they will have to read a great deal of the dreaded book again when they revise for their exams.

Others write notes in the margin. This is a little bit better as a strategy for getting higher marks, but marginalia usually make the most sense only in context, so this messy method also forces the student to reread a great deal of the text.

What is the most effective way to read and remember your textbooks?

The importance of outlining

Outlining a textbook, article or other secondary source is a little bit like what the Japanese call 'reverse engineering' – a way of developing a diagram for something so that you can see exactly how it has been put together. Seeing how published authors build their arguments and marshal their research will help you when it is time to write your own essays.

Seeing that logic of construction will also help you a great deal in remembering the book – by putting the author's points down in your own words, you will be building a way to retrieve the key points of the book more easily from your memory.

Also, outlining will force you to distinguish the most important points from those of secondary importance, helping you build a true understanding of the topic.

Do like the Romans do

Standard outlines use Roman numerals (I, II, III, etc), capital letters, Arabic numerals (1, 2, 3, 4, etc), and lower-case letters and indentations to show relationship and importance of topics in the text. While you certainly do not have to use the Roman numeral system, your outline should be organised in the following manner.

Title
Author

I. First important topic in the text
  A. First subtopic
    1. First subtopic of A
      a. First subtopic of 1
      b. Second subtopic of 1
    2. Second subtopic of A
II. The second important topic in the text

Get the idea? In a book, the Roman numerals would usually refer to chapters; the capital letters to subheadings; and the Arabic numbers and lower-case letters to blocks of paragraphs. In an article or single chapter, the Roman numbers would correspond to subheadings, capital letters to blocks of paragraphs, Arabic numerals to paragraphs and small letters to key sentences.

The discipline of creating outlines will help you home in on the most important points an author is making and capture them, process them and then retain them.

Sometimes an author will put the major point of a paragraph in the first sentence. But just as often the main idea of a paragraph or section will follow some of these tell-tale words: 'therefore', 'because', 'thus', 'since', 'as a result'.

When we see these words we should identify the material they introduce as the major points in our outline. The material immediately preceding and following will almost always be in support of these major points. The outline is an extraordinary tool for organising your thoughts and your time.

Create a timeline

I always found it frustrating to read textbooks in social studies. I would go through chapters on France and the Far East, and have a fairly good understanding of those areas, but have no idea where certain events stood in a global context. As more and more colleges add multicultural curricula, you may find it even more difficult to 'connect' events in 17th-century France or 19th-century Africa with what was happening in the rest of the world.

An excellent tool for overcoming that difficulty is a timeline that you can update periodically. It will help you visualise the chronology and remember the relationship of key world events.

A simple, abridged timeline of Charles Dickens's literary life would look like this. (I suggest you create a horizontal timeline, but the layout of this book makes reproducing it that way difficult, so here is a vertical version.)

1812	Birth
1836	First book published (*Sketches by Boz*)
1837	*Pickwick Papers*
1838	*Oliver Twist*
1850	*David Copperfield*
1853	*Bleak House*
1857	*Little Dorrit*
1861	*Great Expectations*
1870	Death

This makes it easy to see that he was born in the year Napoleon invaded Russia and died soon after the end of the American Civil War. If you added other literary figures from the same period, you would not soon forget that Dickens, Anthony Trollope, Tolstoy, Kierkegaard, Ibsen, Thackeray, Longfellow, Melville and Hawthorne, among many others, were all literary contemporaries. Adding non-literary events to your timeline would enable you to make connections between what was being written and what was going on in the United States, Britain, Europe, Africa, etc.

Draw a concept tree

Another excellent device for limiting the number of words in your notes and making them more memorable is the concept tree. Like a timeline, the concept tree is a visual representation of the relationship among several key facts. For instance, one might depict the categories and examples of musical instruments this way.

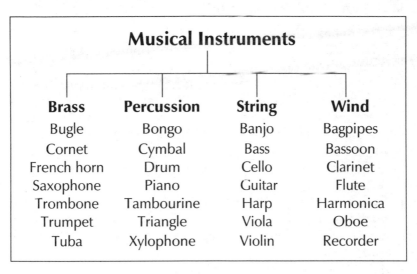

Brass	**Percussion**	**String**	**Wind**
Bugle	Bongo	Banjo	Bagpipes
Cornet	Cymbal	Bass	Bassoon
French horn	Drum	Cello	Clarinet
Saxophone	Piano	Guitar	Flute
Trombone	Tambourine	Harp	Harmonica
Trumpet	Triangle	Viola	Oboe
Tuba	Xylophone	Violin	Recorder

Now we can give credence to the old saying, 'A picture is worth a thousand words', as timelines and concept trees will be much more helpful than mere words in remembering material, particularly conceptual material. Developing them will ensure that your interest in the text will not flag too much.

Add a vocabulary list

Many questions on exam papers require students to define the terminology in a particular discipline. Your physics lecturer will want to know what vectors are, your calculus teacher will want to know about differential equations, your history tutor will want you to be well versed on the Cold War, and your English literature teacher will expect you to know about the romantic poets.

As you read your textbook, make sure you write down all the new terms that seem important and their definitions. I used to draw a box around terms and definitions in my notes, because I knew these were among the most likely items to be asked about and the box would always draw my attention to them when I was reviewing.

Wait, you haven't finished yet

After you have finished taking notes on a chapter, go through them and identify the most important points, either with an asterisk or a highlighter. You will probably end up marking about 40–50 per cent of your entries. When you are reviewing for an exam, you should read all of the notes, but your asterisks will indicate which points you considered the most important while the chapter was still fresh in your mind.

To summarise, when it comes to taking notes from your texts or other reading material, you should:

▮ Take a cursory look through the chapter before you begin reading. Look for subheads, highlighted terms and summaries at the end of the chapter to give you a sense of the content.

▮ Read each section thoroughly. While your review of the chapter 'clues' will help you understand the material, you should read for comprehension rather than speed.

▮ Take notes immediately after you have finished reading, using mapping, the outline, timeline, concept tree and vocabulary list methods of organisation as necessary.

▮ Mark with an asterisk or highlight the key points as you review your notes.

Notes on library materials

At some time during your secondary school, college or university years, you will undoubtedly be called upon to do some extensive research, either for a termly assignment or some other major project. Such a task will be a major undertaking. Note-taking will be only one aspect of the process, albeit an important one.

(While I give you a good system for taking notes for a termly essay or assignment in this chapter, you could also read *Improve Your Writing*, another book in this series, which covers thoroughly all the important steps for producing a written assignment.)

As you will discover, writing a termly assignment will need you to take notes from a number of sources, most of them available at the library. But the more periodicals, reference books and even microfiche you uncover as excellent sources of information for your project, the more likely you will be told that you cannot take these materials out of the library. You will have to take your notes at the library, not at your leisure in the comfort of your room.

So you definitely want a note-taking system that is quick, thorough, efficient and precludes the necessity of having to return to the source. What is the answer?

No, it is not photocopying.

Why photocopying is redundant

You have found a resource that is perfect for your assignment. Your first impulse might be to find the library photocopying machine and start copying.

Is photocopying a help or a hindrance?

I used to employ a system of photocopying when preparing for my term essays. I would go to the library with nothing except a bag of change (photocopying was a lot cheaper in those days), and comb the card catalogue, the shelves and the periodicals index for possible sources, using the library-supplied pencils to write the information down on post-its. I would stack the volumes and periodicals around me at one of the tables and comb through them for hours, looking for juicy quotes and fun facts.

I would mark the books with post-its. Then, I would haul all of the useful sources over to the photocopier and begin photocopying away my hard-earned money.

I would end up going home with a pile of photocopies that I had to reread, which I would do armed with pens of as many different colours as I could find. I would underline all of the related passages with the same colour, pick up another pen and go sifting through the photocopies again. This method certainly helped me produce some very good essays, but it also ensured that I spent too much time rereading information, organising and reorganising the research before I ever began actually writing.

I am about to save you a lot of grief by letting you in on one of the greatest card tricks you have ever seen. And, by the way, you will not ever have to queue for the photocopying machine at the library again.

A great indexing system

Index cards will cut the time it takes to research and organise an essay in half. This is how they work.

Developing a preliminary outline is an important early step in the essay-writing process. Assuming you have completed this step, you then need to be prepared to gather information for your essay or research project. Go to your local stationery shop and buy a supply of 3 x 5 inch index cards.

As you review each source, you will discover some are packed with helpful information, while others may have no useful material at all. Once you have decided that you will use a source, make a working bibliography card:

▌ **In the upper right-hand corner of the card**: write the library book number (Dewey decimal number), or any other detail that will help you locate the material ('Science Reading Room,' 'Main Shelves, 3rd Floor', etc).

▌ **On the main part of the card**: write the author's name, if one is given, last name first. Include the title of the article, if applicable, and write and underline the name of the book, magazine or other publication. Include any other details, such as date of publication, edition, volume number or page numbers where the article or information was found.

▪ **In the upper left-hand corner**: number the card – the card for the first source you plan to use, for example, is No 1, the second is No 2 and so on. If you accidentally miss a number or end up not using a source for which you have filled out a card, do not worry. It is only important that you assign a different number to each card.

▪ **At the bottom of the card**: write the name of the library (if you are researching at more than one) at which you found the source.

By filling out a card for each source, you have just created your working bibliography – a listing of all your sources that will be an invaluable tool when you have to prepare the final bibliography for your essay.

Shuffling cards is a good deal

With index cards, you can organise your list of resources in different ways, just by shuffling the pack.

For example, you might want to start by organising your cards by resource: magazine articles, encyclopaedias, books, newspapers, etc. Then, when you are in the magazine room of the library, you will have a quick and easy way to make sure you read all your magazine articles at the same time. The same goes for your visit to the newspaper reading room, the reference shelf and so on.

However, at some point, you may want to have your list of resources organised in alphabetical order or separated into piles of resources you have checked and those you have not. No problem, just shuffle your cards again.

Even with the help of a computer, it would be very time consuming to do all of this on paper. The note card system is neater and more efficient, and that is the key to getting your work done as quickly and painlessly as possible.

I guarantee you will win this card game

You are sitting in the library now, surrounded by a veritable bonanza of source materials for your paper. You have completed your bibliography cards. It is time to take notes, and this is how to do it.

■ **Write one thought, idea, quote or fact – and only one – on each card.** There are no exceptions. If you encounter a very long quote or string of data, you can write on both the front and back of the card, if necessary. But never carry a note to a second card. If you have an uncontrollable urge to do that, the quote is too long. If you feel that the author is making an incredibly good point, paraphrase it.

■ **Write in your own words**. Do not copy material word for word – you may inadvertently end up plagiarising when you write. Summarise key points or restate the material in your own words.

■ **Put quotation marks around any material copied verbatim**. Sometimes an author makes a point so perfectly, so poetically, you do want to capture it exactly as is. It is fine to do this on a limited basis. But when you do so, you must copy such statements exactly – every sentence, every word, every comma should be exactly as written in the original. And make sure you put quotation marks around this material. Do not rely on your memory to recall, later, which copy was paraphrased and which you copied verbatim.

■ **Put the number of the corresponding bibliography card in the upper left-hand corner**. This is the exact same number you put in the upper left-hand corner of the bibliography card.

■ **Include the page numbers (where you found the information) on the card**. You can add this information under the resource number.

■ **Write down the topic letter that corresponds to your preliminary outline**. For example, the second section, 'B', of your preliminary outline is about the French withdrawal from Vietnam. You found an interesting quote from a United States official that refers to this withdrawal. Write down the topic letter 'B' in the upper right-hand corner of your note card. (You might come across interesting quotes or statistics that could add flavour and authority to your assignment, but you are not quite sure where they will fit in. Mark the card with an asterisk or other symbol instead. Later, when you have a more detailed outline, you may discover where it fits.)

▌ **Give it a headline**. Next to the topic letter, add a brief description of the information on the card. For example, your note card about the French withdrawal may read, 'French withdrawal: US comments'.

As you fill out your note cards, make sure you transfer all information accurately. Always double-check names, dates and other statistics. The beauty of using the note card system is that, once you have captured the information you need, you should never have to return to any of the sources a second time.

A note of caution here: while this system is excellent for helping you organise your time and your material, do not let it thwart you if you find other interesting material.

As with the other exercises in note-taking, the index card system needs you not just to be a transcriber – you could have used the photocopier for that – but a processor of information.

Constantly ask yourself questions while looking at the source material, for example:

Is the author saying this in such a way that I want to quote her directly, or should I paraphrase the material?

If you decide to paraphrase, you obviously do not have to write down the author's exact words, and, therefore, can resort to some of the note-taking tips discussed in other chapters. The answer to this question will have a big impact on how much time it takes to fill in each index card.

Does this material support or contradict the arguments or facts of another author?

Who do I believe? If there is contradictory evidence, should I note it? Can I refute it? If it supports the material I already have, is it interesting or redundant?

Where does this material fit into my outline?

Often, source material will not be as sharply delineated as your plan for the assignment, which is why it is important to place one and only one thought on each card. Even though an author might place more than one thought into a paragraph, or even a sentence, you will be able to stick to your organisational guns if you keep your cards close to your original outline ideas.

You will be super organised

Before I came up with any essay research system in secondary school, my student life was, quite literally, a mess. I had pages and pages of notes for assignments, but sometimes I was unsure where quotes came from and whether or not they were direct quotes or paraphrases.

My photocopying system was not much of an improvement. Often, I would forget one piece of the bibliographic information I needed, necessitating yet another last-minute trip to the library. Organising the voluminous notes when it came time to put my thoughts in order was worse than the researching and writing itself.

The card system will save you all of that effort. Writing one thought, idea, quote, etc, on each card will eliminate the problems caused when unrelated pieces of information appear on the same piece of paper. And writing the number of the source down before doing anything else will help you avoid any problems relating to proper attribution.

When you are ready to do your final outline, all you will need to do is organise and reorder your cards until you have the most effective flow

This simple note card system is, in fact, one that many professional writers – including this one – swear by long after they leave the world of essays and project assignments behind.

Index